Zuzana Poláčková & Pieter C. van Duin

Portugal and Slovakia in Comparative Perspective

Essays on Iberian-Slavic political, social, and cultural questions

With a foreword by Dr. Slavomír Michálek

Reviewers: Josette Baer, Juraj Marušiak
The monograph is the partial result of the following projects: APVV-20-0333 : Prekračovanie hraníc. Fenomén mobility v dejinách Slovenska / (Crossing the frontiers. The Phenomenon of Mobility in the History of Slovakia; VEGA 2/0087/21 Slovensko v 60. rokoch 20. storočia a v období normalizácie. Domáci vývoj a jeho zahranično-politické súvislosti /Slovakia in the 1960s and during the era of normalisation. Domestic developments and their foreign policy context.

Zuzana Poláčková & Pieter C. van Duin

PORTUGAL AND SLOVAKIA IN COMPARATIVE PERSPECTIVE

Essays on Iberian-Slavic political, social, and cultural questions

With a foreword by Dr. Slavomír Michálek

Bibliografische Information der Deutschen Nationalbibliothek
Die Deutsche Nationalbibliothek verzeichnet diese Publikation in der Deutschen Nationalbibliografie; detaillierte bibliografische Daten sind im Internet über http://dnb.d-nb.de abrufbar.

Bibliographic information published by the Deutsche Nationalbibliothek
Die Deutsche Nationalbibliothek lists this publication in the Deutsche Nationalbibliografie; detailed bibliographic data are available in the Internet at http://dnb.d-nb.de.

Cover pictures: ID 192818150 © Aesace | Dreamstime.com.
ID 158591781 © Artem Merzlenko | Dreamstime.com.
ID 30640933 © Dwnld777 | Dreamstime.com

ISBN-13: 978-3-8382-1771-0
© *ibidem*-Verlag, Stuttgart 2023
Alle Rechte vorbehalten

Das Werk einschließlich aller seiner Teile ist urheberrechtlich geschützt. Jede Verwertung außerhalb der engen Grenzen des Urheberrechtsgesetzes ist ohne Zustimmung des Verlages unzulässig und strafbar. Dies gilt insbesondere für Vervielfältigungen, Übersetzungen, Mikroverfilmungen und elektronische Speicherformen sowie die Einspeicherung und Verarbeitung in elektronischen Systemen.

All rights reserved. No part of this publication may be reproduced, stored in or introduced into a retrieval system, or transmitted, in any form, or by any means (electronical, mechanical, photocopying, recording or otherwise) without the prior written permission of the publisher. Any person who does any unauthorized act in relation to this publication may be liable to criminal prosecution and civil claims for damages.

Printed in the EU

Foreword

It does not happen very often that material on Slovak history is used to carry out an exercise in comparative history writing by including historical observations on other European countries. But this is what the essays presented below are doing and I suppose that many Slovak historians will be surprised by the result. Comparative history writing is not something that is practised by many historians in Slovakia and in Portugal the situation is probably not much different, even though in Lisbon some comparative studies have been undertaken in a cultural and literary (but not necessarily historical) context. That the essays also include material on Spain and the Czech lands, indeed even on Brazil, makes them even more ambitious.

It is interesting that the authors of these essays pay attention both to the early modern period and to the twentieth century. The suggestion is that there are historical parallels between Portugal and Slovakia over a longer period of time. Of course there are also historical differences between the two countries, but a case can be made for the thesis that looking at the parallels helps to clarify certain historical questions or even the historical process in the two countries as a whole. However, there were few direct contacts between Portugal and Spain on the one hand and Slovakia or the Czech lands on the other hand. Only when Spanish or Spanish-Italian soldiers were sent to Central Europe to help suppress the Protestant Reformation there, or when Slovak and Hungarian Protestant ministers were sent to the Spanish galleys in Italy, was there a direct contact, in this case of a rather negative kind. The other topics examined in these essays try to draw parallels between historical developments in Portugal or the Iberian world and in Slovakia or Central Europe. One gets the impression that in various historical fields focusing on these parallels is a helpful method even if it is not always easy to do so.

Examples of drawing illuminating parallels are the essay on women and the essay on messianism, Vieira, and Komenský. In both the Iberian Peninsula and Slovakia women were not always helpless in the face of witchcraft accusations. They could manipulate the accusations or intimidate other people by confirming they were witches with special powers.

The last three essays analyse political developments in Portugal and Slovakia in the twentieth century. The deterioration of political Catholicism to a form of semi-fascism happened in both countries and was the result both of internal tendencies within this movement itself and of external developments, including political chaos in Portugal and the domination of liberal secularists in Czechoslovakia. It is remarkable that in both countries the historical factor of Catholicism played a crucial role in cultural, social, and political developments. At the same time, however, communism was an important movement too. Both in Portugal and Slovakia the influence of communist ideology remains a notable fact.

Dr Slavomír Michálek, DrSc ,
Director of the Institute of History;
of the Slovak Academy of Sciences,
Bratislava.

Table of Contents

Preface 11

1. History, politics, and 'multiculturalism': Portugal and
   Slovakia compared 17

   Portugal until the mid-nineteenth century 19

   Slovakia until c. 1850 22

   Portugal and Slovakia since the later nineteenth century 25

   Politics and the legacy of dictatorship 28

   Ethno-national and 'multicultural' problems compared 32

   Conclusions 37

2. Gender, power, and social disciplining: comparative
   observations on the position of women in early modern
   Slovakia and the Iberian Peninsula 41

   Religion, culture, and education 42

   Contours and background of the witch-craze 46

   Problems of social disciplining, community conflict, and
   witchcraft 50

   'Melancholy' and imagined power: contradictory
   tendencies 55

3. Iberian images and personalities of the Counter-
   Reformation in Slavic Central Europe 59

   The challenge of Slavic and Hungarian Protestantism 60

   Spanish Catholic tyranny and Italian paradoxes 61

   'Iberians' in Central Europe and their image 63

   Antonio Caraffa and the 'Prešov slaughterhouse' 66

   Conclusions 68

4. Disaster and salvation: Jan Amos Komenský (1592-1670), António Vieira (1608-1697), and the meanings of seventeenth-century messianism 71

   Missionary movements and messianic thought: a closer look 74

   The messianic dynamics, religious and secular 77

   Komenský, Vieira, and the seventeenth century 80

   Concluding observations 82

5. The miracle of Maurício: multicultural toleration and decolonising tendencies in seventeenth-century Brazil 85

   Seventeenth-century Brazil 89

   'Divine justice will intervene' 93

   Peculiarities of Dutch Brazil 98

   A chaotic unravelling 104

   Concluding observations 109

6. Portugal, Slovakia and the political Counter-Reformation of the twentieth century (1910-1939) 113

   Introduction 114

   Portugal 117

   A conservative revolution 125

   Slovakia 130

   Catholicism, nationalism, authoritarianism 136

   Conclusions 143

7. Authoritarianism in crisis: Portugal, Czechoslovakia, and '1968' 149

   Portugal: the last phase of right-wing authoritarianism 151

   Czechoslovakia: crisis, reform, and the restoration of communist authoritarianism 164

   Conclusions 181

8. Slovakia and Portugal 1989-1993: changing political cultures and communist movements compared 185

    The Portuguese scene 186

    The Slovak scene 189

About the authors 195

Preface

The idea to explore comparative dimensions of the history and cultures of the Iberian and Slavic nations was originally conceived and developed at the Faculty of Literature of the University of Lisbon and by the International Society for Iberian-Slavonic Studies shortly after 2000. Since then, annual conferences on various cross-cultural and interdisciplinary topics held in Lisbon have inspired a growing number of researchers in the linguistic, cultural, and historical fields, hailing from Portugal, Spain, Poland, Slovakia, the Czech Republic, Serbia, Slovenia, Scotland, the Netherlands, Brazil, and the United States. The authors of the present collection of essays figured among them, and we accumulated over time a number of unpublished papers based on our contributions to the Lisbon conferences. It was certainly helpful that our research was honoured and supported by the Instituto Camoes and the Portuguese Embassy in Bratislava. During the pandemic of 2020-21 we decided to bring out eight essays in a small publication with the aim of offering some examples of comparative Iberian-Slavic historical research. This, of course, is also meant to be a contribution to European history. While our more specific focus is on Portuguese-Slovak comparative questions, our collection also touches topics relating to Spain, the Czech lands, Italy, and Brazil. The inclusion of essay no. 5 on Brazil, originally written for a conference at Aveiro in Portugal, is justified because of its connection to the colonial concerns and activities of António Vieira (see essay no. 4) and the wide-ranging issue of 'multiculturalism'. In the case of Portugal, of course, the latter is closely associated with the country's historic colonialism and more recent 'post-colonial' challenges. Additionally, a historic variant of this issue persists in the shape of ethno-linguistic and nationality differences in Central and South Eastern European countries like Slovakia, Romania, and Bosnia.

Thus, while the Slovak-Portuguese comparison is our key subject, the comparative investigations presented in these essays are carried out on diverse geographic and historical levels. On the one hand we are concerned with Portugal, Spain, the Iberian Peninsula as a whole, or Iberia's European and American extensions; on the other hand with Slovakia, the Czech lands, the former Czechoslovakia, or Slavic Central Europe. The dimension of comparison and parallel histories predominates over the dimension of direct historical or cultural contact in whatever form. Essay no. 3 is the only essay which investigates a special case of Iberian-Slavic historical contact, even though it concerns an indirect rather than a direct and a violent rather than a peaceful form of contact. In addition, there is a relatively strong focus on topics from the seventeenth and the twentieth century. The sixteenth, eighteenth, and nineteenth centuries are not absent, however, but included in several comparative accounts in some of the essays. The strong presence of the seventeenth and twentieth centuries is the result of our research activities in recent years and does not mean that we regard other periods as less important or less interesting. It is clear that much work remains to be done if we are to arrive at a more complete picture of Portuguese-Slovak or Iberian-Slavic comparative history, and a historiography truly covering the broadest possible range of topics.

The three fields of historical inquiry explicitly mentioned in the title of this collection are the political, social, and cultural ones. They are represented in these essays in diverse forms and contexts. The history of European politics, of course, refers to power structures, political ideologies, and different forms of conflict, among others. The social sphere relates to the role and position of different (types of) social groups and different patterns of inequality, stratification, and socio-cultural group distinction, i.e. a whole range of social issues including economic inequality on one side and ethnic or religious inequality on the other. Indeed, forms of vertical (e.g. economic or gender) stratification and horizontal (e.g. linguistic or national) segmentation often existed side by side in the same social system. The cultural sphere is perhaps the most complex and the most difficult to come to grips with, in the context of European, colonial, and comparative world history. It relates to the ideological, religious, and 'mental' domains per se and to all sorts of socio-psychological phenomena including mutual group prejudices, stigmatisation of marginalised people, and the cultivation of all sorts of stereotypical images and ideas. These are old phenomena in

European history — from anti-Judaism to marginalisation of women to colonial racism — but they have taken on a new urgency and, perhaps, more articulated features in the twentieth century with its increasingly conscious reflection on cross-cultural and 'multicultural' problems. There is hardly an essay in this collection in which these issues do not figure in one way or another. Arguably, over the course of five or more centuries there was not only a European experience of political, socio-economic, and cultural change, but also a dimension of continuity in terms of the salience of multicultural questions in this overwhelmingly Christian yet simultaneously fragmented continent. Problems of inter-Christian, ethno-national, and political-ideological controversy shaped the history of Europe even if the terms of debate were partly modified over time.

After these general remarks, a brief introductory description of the eight essays seems useful. Essay no. 1 offers a concise overview of some of the major questions in Portuguese and Slovak history from the fifteenth to the early twenty-first century. It shows both historical differences and similarities between the two countries with the former being rather obvious (maritime and early independent Portugal vs. landlocked and long dependent Slovakia) and the latter proving quite significant. Above all, the dominant role of Catholicism (the initially successful Reformation among the Slovaks notwithstanding) had important consequences for Portugal and Slovakia. Their experience in the twentieth century included a political modernisation of conservative and authoritarian Catholicism, which is further analysed in essay no. 6.

Essay no. 2 examines and compares historical phenomena on the Iberian Peninsula and in Slovakia (Upper Hungary) relating to the position of women in the early modern period. Although it is clear that women were marginalised in many ways, it seems undeniable that not only the more educated but also some 'ordinary' or marginalised women were able to put up resistance against those who denounced them, or, paradoxically, to exploit threatening situations including witchcraft accusations to increase their prestige. In some cases, accusations of sorcery could be appropriated by the accused to 'prove' their magic powers and intimidate others — even though this usually resulted in permanent isolation and exacerbated existing tensions and conflicts with the rest of the community. Interestingly, this issue of 'the power of the powerless' also emerges in the very different context of colonial Brazil (essay no. 5).

Essay no. 3 focuses on the involvement of 'Iberian' or 'Hispanic' actors and symbols in some of the military and political events of the Counter-Reformation in Central Europe. The personalities in question contributed to the emergence or confirmation of anti-Catholic images in the Czech lands and Slovakia, regions where Protestantism had become an influential cultural and political factor by the early seventeenth century. Through the 'mediation' of men from Spanish-ruled Naples and Milan, Czech, Slovak, and Magyar Protestants were directly confronted with what was seen as the uniquely brutal methods of oppression by the Iberian Catholic superpower. This could only amplify the negative images associated with the 'Black Legend' of Spanish cruelty.

Essay no. 4 on Komenský, Vieira, and 'messianism' argues that, despite all the differences between the leader of the Czech Brethren and the prominent Portuguese Jesuit, the similarities between them are remarkable and fascinating. Both men believed in the necessity of human action to improve the moral, religious, and political condition of the world. At the same time both of them were convinced that such human action could not succeed without divine help and intervention, or rather, that it could only bring the required and desired transformation when it fitted into the wider scheme of things, i.e. divine providence and the preordained course of salvation history. It becomes clear that this frame of thought was part of both the older Catholic and the new Protestant way of looking at the world. What united Christian thinkers and idealists like Komenský and Vieira was an established Christian pattern, which existed both in Iberia and Slavic Central Europe.

Essay no. 5 shows that the world of Western Christianity had come to comprise the American continent as well. But how does an essay on Brazil fit in with Portuguese-Slavic or Iberian-Slavic comparative studies? Clearly, the culture and identity of Portugal are difficult to understand without including its colonial experience and spectacular overseas extension. A man like António Vieira was active both in Brazil and in Portugal and his role in protecting indigenous Brazilians is well known. Vieira, and others with similar critical and messianic ideas, attached a special significance to the Dutch invasion of seventeenth-century Brazil and the rule of Governor Johan Maurits of Nassau, known in Brazil as 'Maurício'. Both could be seen as a divine punishment for the sins of the Portuguese, as several Catholic friars including Vieira were arguing. An examination of colonial Brazil's multicultural complexity is also helpful from a heuristic and comparative point of view, viz. to help interpret some of Europe's social and cultural problems.

Essay no. 6 explores the thesis that twentieth-century political Catholicism in Portugal and Slovakia evolved into a conservative movement that can be interpreted as a secularised continuation of the Counter-Reformation. Of course, in both countries there were more progressive Catholics as well, but they were a minority that could not decisively influence the course of events leading to dictatorship and a semi-fascist ideological worldview. While in Portugal the right-wing dictatorship survived until 1974, in Slovakia (Czechoslovakia) it was succeeded by a left-wing dictatorship, i. e. Soviet-imposed communism, after 1945. It is a challenge for historians to compare the two anti-democratic systems and their crises, and to do so by taking national historical contexts into account while simultaneously looking at authoritarian parallels.

Essay no. 7 takes on this challenge, even though on the 'Slavic side' the subject of comparison is socialist Czechoslovakia rather than Slovakia. The year 1968 was a fateful one for both countries, and, quite apart from international dynamics, an examination of the political conditions prevailing in Portugal and Czechoslovakia can explain why. Factors like elite disunity, declining fear among the population, weakening of ideological legitimacy, and reformist efforts to make the authoritarian system less rigid and more viable shaped a process of change through which it eventually collapsed.

Essay no. 8 examines what happened to the communist movements in Portugal and Slovakia after 1989. Although there were strong post-authoritarian and democratic tendencies in Czechoslovak communism and even in the rather doctrinaire and semi-Stalinist Portuguese Communist Party, a group of more rigid and conservative communists survived in the 1990s as well. This was almost inevitable in Portugal, given the leading role of hardliner Cunhal. But old-fashioned communism — rather surprisingly — also remained a factor of some significance in Slovakia. Looking at the memoirs of an old Slovak communist (and natural scientist) provides some insight into the communist way of thinking. Both the latter and the right-wing authoritarian mind-set have by no means disappeared from Europe, whose democratic political culture can never be taken for granted.

Thus, we present eight essays with four of them focusing mainly on the seventeenth century, three on the twentieth century, and essay number 1 on a more general comparative overview. The eighteenth and nineteenth centuries are examined as well — especially in essays number 1, 2 and 6, as already noted. We hope that other historians will be interested to help fill the many gaps that remain.

1. History, politics, and 'multiculturalism': Portugal and Slovakia compared

This essay puts forward a comparative analysis of Portugal and Slovakia as European nations from a modern historical, contemporary political, and 'multicultural' perspective. Thus, not only the differences but also certain similarities between the two countries can be illuminated. The historical perspective shows several parallels between Portugal and Slovakia, for example the strong position of the Catholic Church and the problems in introducing social, cultural, and political reforms. A political analysis of developments in the twentieth century shows that both nations struggled with the implementation of policies of democratic modernisation, with Portugal falling prey to an authoritarian regime with fascist overtones and Slovakia experiencing a similar form of what has been called 'clerical fascism', followed by the yoke of communist dictatorship. As a consequence, both countries are still suffering from a legacy of 'democratic deficit', although Slovakia probably more so than Portugal.

Another interesting aspect of the social, cultural, and political profile of present-day Portugal and Slovakia is the issue of multicultural problems and multi-ethnic population structure. In both countries this is a critical feature of the contemporary political and socio-cultural landscape. Whereas in Portugal the issue is mainly the result of mass immigration from the country's former colonies, in Slovakia it principally relates to the older problems of the status of the Hungarian minority and the social integration of the substantial Roma population. A comparison of these two variants of 'multicultural problematic' is a challenging task for both historians and social and political scientists.

Any attempt to examine Portugal and Slovakia in the same context and to look for the most significant similarities and differences between them may seem at first sight a somewhat far-fetched undertaking. Many people would probably see no political, cultural, or historical parallels between the two countries at all, and would regard a comparative analysis of them as a waste of time. But this assumption is wrong. What Portugal and Slovakia have in common is first of all the plain fact that both nations belong to Europe and that they share a common European history in the broadest sense of the word. Their role and specific position within this broader European history may have been rather different over the course of five centuries, but both nations made a special contribution to it and shared a number of common European experiences in the cultural, religious, economic, and political sphere. Moreover, at the end of the twentieth century both Portugal and Slovakia became part of a new European experience: the endeavour to create a new form of European unity and to make all European nations participate in the project of ensuring stability and prosperity for the people of Europe as a whole.

We want to look at Portugal and Slovakia in three ways: by examining differences and parallels between their histories as European nations; by analysing their political experience especially in the tragic and contradictory twentieth century; and by looking at the specific issue of the position of ethnic, national, and socio-cultural minorities in both countries, i.e. the fact that both Portugal and Slovakia are, at least to some extent, 'multicultural' and ethnically heterogeneous states. The first dimension is important enough in its own right and must provide the necessary historical background to any attempt to understand the present-day reality of Portugal or Slovakia. The second dimension may help us understand why both countries had many difficulties in achieving more democratic political conditions in the twentieth century, and why both of them rank among those European nations which had to make a special effort to consolidate their newly won democratic system and develop a democratic political culture. The third dimension will give us more insight into the cultural complexity of Portuguese and Slovak society as both nations strive to 'synthesise' a European orientation, an older national consciousness, and the new reality of having to integrate minorities, some of whom are (seen as) groups with a different and perhaps 'problematic' identity. The 'European project', 'national identity', and 'multicultural reality' are interrelated in complex and sometimes surprising ways.

Portugal until the mid-nineteenth century

The role of Portugal in European history is in some ways quite unique. The country was the first in Europe to embark on the project of maritime and colonial expansion with the aim of exploring new trade routes and developing new ways of gaining profit from them. This trend already started in the fourteenth century and was in some ways a continuation of Portugal's (and Spain's) struggle against Islam and the dominant Islamic powers of the late medieval era. Portugal's capital Lisbon soon became the largest and richest trading hub in Europe, displaying convincing proof of the success of Portuguese overseas activities. It is interesting that, while Portugal and Spain became the most dynamic nations of fifteenth- and sixteenth-century Europe, both countries persistently adhered to their Catholic faith. Other nations who began to play a role on the world stage somewhat later in the sixteenth century — notably England and the Dutch Republic — experienced Protestant revolutions, which helped to give their societies a more 'modern' political, social, and cultural profile by the seventeenth century. The reason why Portugal always remained so consistently and conservatively Catholic was probably that the Catholic religion and the Catholic Church had become a hallmark of its national identity during the long struggle against Islam. The deeply rooted Catholic identity was bound to remain a crucial cultural feature of Portugal,[1] despite the emergence of an anti-clerical countermovement in the eighteenth and nineteenth centuries.

The fact that this Catholic rigidity could also become a source of weakness and internal division was shown, for example, by the remarkable Portuguese intolerance of the Jews, including those who had converted to Christianity under pressure. The Jews were an important economic group in late-medieval and sixteenth-

---

[1] See for the question of Catholic identity in Portugal and the relationship between religious and national identity A. Matos Ferreira, 'Nação e religião: identidade e contradições', pp. 105-18, and Manuel Clemente, 'Catolicismo e identidade portuguesa', pp. 119-32, both in H. Fernandes, I. Castro Henriques, J. da Silva Horta, and S. Campos Matos (eds.), *Nação e Identidades. Portugal, os Portugueses e os Outros* (Lisbon, 2009).

century Portugal, but by increasingly suppressing them and finally driving most of them out of the country the Portuguese were arguably acting against their own economic interests.[2] It was difficult for the nation that pioneered the economic and scientifically underpinned transatlantic and global expansion of Europe to develop a more rational and tolerant attitude towards cultural and religious issues. Many wealthy Portuguese Jews eventually moved to North Africa and the Ottoman Empire but also to the new European power, the Dutch Republic, which became a major competitor of Portugal in overseas trade and maritime expansion by using, among other things, the expertise and financial resources of Jewish and other refugees from more intolerant countries in Europe.

Between 1580 and 1640 Portugal was incorporated as part of the Kingdom of Spain. This 'dark period' in Portuguese history was a significant reason for the Portuguese people to define their nation in opposition to Spain.[3] It most likely also contributed to the move towards greater isolation from all enemies and competitors. A pragmatic exception was made for England, which had begun to act long ago as the protector and ally of Portugal in her endeavours to remain politically independent and keep the Spanish at bay. At the end of the seventeenth century gold was found in Brazil, and during the eighteenth century the Portuguese monarchy, aristocracy, and the Catholic Church took advantage of this new source of wealth to strengthen their traditionally powerful position and to carry out a number of rather ostentatious architectural projects

---

[2] See Yosef Hayim Yerushalmi, 'Le judaïsme séfarade entre la Croix et le Croissant', pp. 24-31, in his *Sefardica. Essais sur l'histoire des Juifs, des marranes et des nouveaux-chrétiens d'origine hispano-portugaise* (Paris, 1998) for a brief account of the intermittent persecution and expulsion of the Jews since the fourteenth century; see also Esther Benbassa (ed.) et al., *Mémoires juives d'Espagne et du Portugal* (Paris, 1996); David Birmingham, *A Concise History of Portugal* (Cambridge, 2003), Chapters 1-2, passim.

[3] See for the intriguing issue of the Portuguese-Spanish relationship Michael Scotti-Rosin, 'Nahe Ferne oder ferne Nähe: Überlegungen zu einer schwierigen Beziehung', *Lusorama* 59-60 (November 2004), pp. 61-85; for the question of nationalism and national identity also Clare Mar-Molinero and Angel Smith (eds.), *Nationalism and the Nation in the Iberian Peninsula (Competing and Constructing Identities)* (Berg, 1996), especially the introductory chapter by the editors, 'The Myths and Realities of Nation-Building in the Iberian Peninsula', pp. 1-30.

displaying the status and wealth of the ruling strata. This could be seen — and indeed has been seen by historians — as a missed opportunity for Portugal to initiate a new phase of economic modernisation instead of squandering the new resources on prestige projects. Indeed, earlier opportunities and colonial revenue had been wasted as well. The wealth from Brazil and other Portuguese colonies could have been used to start new industries and encourage the development of a stronger national bourgeoisie. But this did not happen and Portugal gave the impression of being stuck in an older age of monarchical, feudal, and Catholic splendour instead of daring to embark upon a new era of national 'regeneration' — a term that became popular in the nineteenth century — and strengthening its competitive power in the arena of the emerging international economy. The country that actually benefited from this was Brazil, which received hundreds of thousands of poor immigrants from Portugal.

As already noted, besides the traditional aristocracy and monarchy, a crucial factor behind Portugal's social and cultural conservatism was the powerful Catholic Church, afraid of all experiments in modernisation that might threaten the existing order. In spite of the age of European Enlightenment, the Portuguese Church was continuing its horrific practice of ritually burning groups of 'heretics' of various descriptions 'to demonstrate that the church was still mightier than the state'.[4] Only the terrible earthquake which destroyed a large part of Lisbon in 1755 and the subsequent reform programme of the enlightened despot Marquis of Pombal were able to lift Portugal to some degree out of its medieval cultural inertia, social and political backwardness, and counterproductive Catholic conservatism. But later in the eighteenth century, after Pombal had lost his influence, some of the reforms were diluted again, though not completely reversed. In the early nineteenth century Portugal was ravaged by war and invasions, first having to fight the French and then, in the national revolution of 1820, the old British 'ally' who had become an occupier of the country. The civil war of the 1830s weakened the country additionally and made it difficult for

---

[4] Birmingham, *A Concise History of Portugal*, p. 69.

the Portuguese to start the modernisation of their political, economic, and cultural institutions. Nevertheless, the country more or less succeeded in this endeavour during the more liberal period from 1820 to 1850.

Slovakia until c. 1850

When we look at the history of Slovakia (Upper Hungary) during the same period — roughly from the fifteenth to the mid-nineteenth century — we observe a number of similarities as well as differences compared to the long-term experience of Portugal.[5] Like Portugal, Slovakia had to deal with an Islamic enemy, in this case the expanding Ottoman Empire in south-east Europe. The ethnic Slovak region was part of the Kingdom of Hungary, one of the oldest state formations in Europe that had been founded around the year 1000, more than a century before the establishment of the Portuguese Kingdom in the early twelfth century. Slovakia as a region of multilingual feudal Hungary did not have any autonomous political institutions; in this respect its position was completely different from independent (and culturally more homogeneous) Portugal. Nevertheless, the Slovak region was seen as a special part of the Hungarian Kingdom and occasionally referred to as 'the Slav Land', the 'land of the Slovaks', and the like. The Slovaks constituted the great majority of the population of this northern Hungarian region and it is acceptable to speak of 'Slovakia' in a historic-ethnographic sense when referring to the period before 1918 — the year when multinational Hungary collapsed and Slovakia became a part of the new Czechoslovak Republic.

The Slovak region became more important for Hungary as a whole, and indeed for the Habsburg Monarchy, within which Hungary became a dependent kingdom in the sixteenth century, after the Ottoman armies conquered central Hungary in 1526. Thus, Slovakia turned into a borderland of what remained of Royal Hungary and found itself a direct neighbour of the Ottoman Empire. Most of

---

[5] See for an English-language history of Slovakia Stanislav J. Kirschbaum, *A history of Slovakia: the struggle for survival* (New York, 1996).

the territory was not occupied by the Turks but rather experienced an endless series of Turkish raids. It was often visited by Central and Western Europeans who wanted to see this civilisational frontier with their own eyes. A second important feature of 16th century Slovakia was a mining industry with relatively developed production methods.

The difference between the Portuguese and the Slovak experience with their respective Islamic enemies was especially one of historical time. While for Portugal the confrontation with Islam near its own territory was over already before 1500 — in contrast to Spain this even had been the case since the thirteenth century — for Slovakia the same kind of experience was about to begin around that time. What Portugal and Slovakia have in common, however, is a historical consciousness in which Islam is seen as a direct threat in political and cultural terms. The question might be posed how far the new European experience with Islam in the early twenty-first century is a factor reviving the old enemy image. But probably the image of Islam as 'the historical enemy' of Christian Europe is a more general one across the European continent. Indeed, the historical image of the "Islamic enemy" persists even today and affects many modern European societies.

Like in Portugal, the Catholic Church in Slovakia is a dominant institution in the history of the country and there can be no doubt that it shaped many of the characteristic cultural traits of the Slovak people that are still visible today. A historical difference, however, is that in Slovakia — and in other parts of the old Hungarian Kingdom — Protestantism survived as a 'secondary' religious and cultural tradition of some importance. This added a degree of pluralism to Slovak culture and society that is missing in the Catholic 'monoculture' of Portugal. But at the same time the Catholic Church was similarly a strong conservative and rather intolerant force in Slovakia. This may have had, in addition to feudalism and other political factors, a significant influence on the relative lack of social and economic — not to mention cultural and political — modernisation that was perceptible in Slovakia and Hungary, similar to the situation in Portugal. Like in Portugal, there were those who tried to implement a programme of cultural and socio-economic modernisation, in particular the great Habsburg emperor Joseph II in the 1780s as well as groups of reform-minded Catholics and Protestants before, during, and after that remarkable decade. But also like in Portugal their initiatives were only partly successful, even if in some fields of cultural and political life changes were introduced that had a lasting impact, including educational reform and a more effective 'anti-clerical' policy restricting the power and influence of the Catholic Church. Thus, on the one hand and similar to Portugal, Slovakia continued to be characterised until the mid-nineteenth century by semi-feudal features in the social, economic, and more traditional cultural spheres. But on the other hand, in the political and intellectual spheres, modern ideological and nationalistic ideas began to influence larger numbers of people and thus foreshadowed the coming of a modern age of democratic and liberal ideals and increased political participation.

During the first half of the nineteenth century attempts were made by a 'national-liberal' and reform-minded section of the Hungarian nobility to introduce economic, social, and cultural reforms. But these initiatives were accompanied by a policy of increasingly systematic 'Magyarisation' (linguistic and national-cultural assimilation) of the non-Magyar populations in Hungary, including the Slovaks, Romanians, Germans, Jews and other ethnic groups who had their own languages, cultural traditions, and even a new sense of separate national identity. This resulted in fierce nationality struggles in multinational Hungary and was one factor among others slowing down the political and economic progress of Hungary as a whole. By the mid-nineteenth century national conflict between the ethnic Hungarians and the other nations of Hungary had become the most critical feature of Slovakia's political and cultural landscape. In this regard, the situation in Slovakia differed from that in Portugal, which was able to profit from its greater cultural and national homogeneity.

Portugal and Slovakia since the later nineteenth century

In Portugal meanwhile, a new 'liberal', ideologically modern, reformist, and partly republican political class had appeared that in some respects was similar to (some of) the Hungarian national-liberal reformers of the nineteenth century. Lawyers and other men belonging to the free professions and the intelligentsia played an increasingly prominent role in this relatively independent group, whose social and political profile might be defined as 'bourgeois' (even if this label is not entirely satisfying). Both the Portuguese and the Hungarian liberal elite—and even the small Slovak elite of national 'awakeners'—were self-conscious political pioneers with a strong sense of the need for a progressive ideology showing the way forward towards national 'modernisation'. This included linking the nation's 'glorious past'—an idea that not only existed in Portugal—to its hopefully glorious future. In this complex ideological context, the Hungarian national-liberal avant-garde—speaking for the Magyars who represented at best half of Hungary's population—came into conflict with the emerging Slovak national intelligentsia, which was creating its own historical myths about the glorious Slav and Slovak past in an attempt to fight back against the national claims of the Magyars. The national ideologies of the Hungarians and the Slovaks can be compared with the national-liberal claims of the new Portuguese political class, which tried to redefine the Portuguese past in a more democratic and increasingly republican way. Its most anti-clerical and radical section rediscovered the great colonial past of the Portuguese nation in its own way, trying to fit it into a 'positivist' (secular and progressive) ideology of Portuguese 'regeneration', national modernisation, and republicanism.[6] At the same time a more conservative and Catholic tendency

---

[6] See for example AbdoolKarim A. Vakil, 'Nationalising Cultural Politics: Representations of the Portuguese "Discoveries" and the Rhetoric of Identitarianism, 1880-1926', pp. 33-52, and Alan Freeland, 'The People and the Poet: Portuguese National Identity and the Camões Tercentenary (1880)', pp. 53-66, both in Mar-Molinero and Smith (eds.), *Nationalism and the Nation in the Iberian Peninsula*. See for different aspects of nineteenth-and early twentieth-century liberalism, anti-

within the Portuguese political landscape presented its own version of the Portuguese past as well, one in which the historic task of spreading Christianity and Roman Catholicism played a major part, in stark contrast to the secular and more 'scientific' and 'economistic' ideology of the anti-clerical liberals, republicans, and socialists.

A similar ideological and cultural-political conflict between 'liberals' and 'Catholics' emerged in late nineteenth-century Hungary, including in Upper Hungary and the Slovak national movement. Also in Slovakia the twentieth century opened with 'cultural struggles' between progressive secularists and conservative Catholics, with both groups beginning to mobilise broader sections of the population even beyond the small middle and lower-middle class. In a sense, the entire 'intra-ethnic' political history of the Slovak nation in the twentieth century was a cultural and ideological confrontation between 'national secularists', including patriotic liberals, democrats, and socialists, on the one hand, and 'national conservatives', including Catholics, conservative Protestants, and even anti-democrats, on the other. Communism as an authoritarian force on the Left helped to weaken the democratic forces within the secular camp as a whole. Many Slovak progressivists wanted political unity with the Czechs in order to more effectively isolate the Catholic and conservative Slovak national camp. In this perspective, the Czechs were seen as a brother nation who could help to modernise — also from a cultural point of view – 'backward' Slovakia. However, many Slovak Catholics and other Slovaks defended the idea of a separate national (including more religious) identity of the Slovaks, fighting after 1918 for Slovak political autonomy within the new Czechoslovak State and against what was seen as a Czechoslovak programme of cultural modernisation and secularisation that contradicted Slovak traditions.

In Portugal the liberals and their allies succeeded in establishing a republic in 1910, which tried to continue the national modernisation project that had begun in the nineteenth century. Their

---

clericalism, and republicanism António Ventura, *Estudos sobre história e cultura contemporâneas de Portugal* (Lisbon, 2004).

weakness was demonstrated by the incomplete success (but not complete failure) of this project and the fact that in 1926 the country experienced another coup d'état. There had been many coups in Portugal ever since the early nineteenth century, but now a military and dictatorial regime came to power with increasingly fascist and reactionary Catholic traits. From 1928 the regime was led by the minister of finance António de Oliveira Salazar, an authoritarian Catholic who gradually increased his power and became the undisputed leader of the country in the 1930s. In the 1920s and 1930s democratic Slovakia witnessed the rise of an authoritarian national-Catholic movement as well, the oppositional Slovak People's Party led by Andrej Hlinka. In 1938 the Party took over the government of Slovakia as Czechoslovakia disintegrated, installing a semi-fascist ('clerical-fascist') regime with Catholic and extreme nationalist overtones that was not much different from its Portuguese counterpart. Thus, there are interesting parallels between the Portuguese and Slovak experiences in the form of authoritarian movements leaning on strong Catholic traditions, with a political mentality that partly overlapped with the ideology and practices of fascism. At the same time, the two cases differ in that the Slovak variant of 'national-Catholic dictatorship' was based on a strong political movement which had been growing 'from below', whereas the Portuguese regime had come to power by a military coup that was largely supported by sections of the political, social, and military elites. And while the Slovak regime was dependent on German support for its survival, its Portuguese counterpart managed to stay in power without outside assistance. At any rate, both countries found it difficult to develop a successful project of democratic modernisation (even apart from outside factors in the Slovak case) and were suffering from a problematical legacy of Catholic conservatism, hierarchical traditions, and weakness of liberal political trends.

These findings open a promising field of more detailed historical, cultural, and political comparisons between the two countries especially with regard to events in the first half of the twentieth century. But there are also some interesting parallels concerning the long-term evolution of Portugal and Slovakia, i.e. during a historical period spanning several centuries. Nevertheless, our comparative historical survey must end at this point. The next section contains additional observations on political developments in the twentieth century, followed by a discussion of 'multicultural' problems.

Politics and the legacy of dictatorship

The experiences that Portugal and Slovakia had with various forms of dictatorship in the twentieth century must be a major topic of historical analysis, and indeed in this respect and in terms of general political context there were similarities as well as differences between the two countries. One difference, as already noted, was that Portugal could more or less decide its own fate without external intervention, facilitated by its longstanding state independence and peripheral geographic position, among other things. In the case of Slovakia, however, the country's location in the heart of East-Central Europe and the historic reality of political dependence meant that the path to autonomy was long and winding. The country was a region within multinational Hungary until 1918 and then became part of the new Czechoslovak State, which was dominated by the Czechs. During the existence of the First Czechoslovak Republic (1918-1938) Slovakia experienced a period of democracy, national-cultural progress, and a degree of economic and social modernisation including a programme of land reform. But there was also de-industrialisation, substantial unemployment, and mass emigration. While Portugal entered a period of self-imposed dictatorship, decline of political culture, and liquidation of democratic freedoms after 1926, Slovakia had its political problems too. The antagonism between Slovak 'progressivists' and Slovak Catholics intensified, and there were also tensions between Slovaks and Czechs. Although the democratic political culture of Czechoslovakia was consolidated and the country's German and Hungarian minorities benefited from the democratic character of the state as well, there were also less promising tendencies among a part of the Slovaks and some political groups representing the national minorities.

National minority problems, including the question of the Hungarian minority in Slovakia, had several negative consequences. In the Slovak-Magyar relationship the tables were turned in 1918 with the 'New Slovakia' now containing a Hungarian minority instead of the Slovaks being a minority nationality in Greater Hungary. This reinforced the mutual suspicion of Slovaks and ethnic Hungarians, a problem that was difficult to overcome especially because the smaller post-1918 Hungary wanted a revision of the new borders in Central Europe and to re-incorporate the Hungarian minorities now living in Slovakia, Romania, and Serbia/Yugoslavia.

This had a destabilising impact on the region, which was exacerbated by the increasingly anti-Czech Slovak political movement led by the Catholic leader Hlinka striving for Slovak autonomy and, it seemed, a political system that was more authoritarian than the Czechoslovak Republic. In the 'Slovak State' led by Hlinka's successor, the Catholic priest Jozef Tiso, from 1938-9, many Slovaks apparently were willing to tolerate a semi-fascist regime as long as conservative 'Catholic' and 'national' values were honoured. The Slovak National Uprising of 1944, however, helped to restore Slovakia's profile to some extent. After World War II the country hardly had time to recuperate from its war experiences or make a new start as a democratic nation. Now it was the communists who were determined to seize power and to impose their own version of dictatorship.

Although Portugal had been suffering under the regime of 'Catholic soldiers' and Salazar since 1926, she had managed to keep out of the Second World War. But this was precisely the reason why its dictatorial regime — similar to the Franco regime in Spain — could survive for the incredibly long period of another thirty years. Although the Portuguese dictatorship ended fifteen years earlier (in 1974) than the communist regime in Czechoslovakia, it had begun some twenty years before the communist take-over in 1945-8. In other words, the Portuguese dictatorship lasted longer than the communist dictatorship in Slovakia.

Some analysts have argued that the dictatorship in Portugal was not a 'fascist' or 'totalitarian' regime in the proper sense of the word. And maybe it is indeed necessary to distinguish between an 'authoritarian' regime (such as the Portuguese one or the Slovak State) and a 'totalitarian' (communist or purely fascist) regime. In this vein, it has been argued by a French analyst that the Portuguese regime was not really fascist—in the Italian or German sense of propagating a comprehensive ideology accompanied by mass mobilisation—but none the less 'totalitarian', 'police-run', and so on.[7] Other historians have come to the conclusion that it was fascist or semi-fascist (in terms of political style and ideological claims) rather than totalitarian (in terms of political and repressive efficiency). However that may be, the most important thing to note is that the Portuguese regime of 1926-1974 was highly oppressive, dictatorial, and intimidating even if it was not completely totalitarian. How to define a regime, for example, that was 'cultivating' rather than suppressing rumours about its torture practices?[8]

The argument that the Portuguese regime was not totalitarian in the sense of liquidating all social and political structures of civil society, in contrast to the communist regime in Slovakia, may be tested by looking at the depth of political, cultural, and socio-economic destruction caused by both dictatorial regimes. In the Portuguese case, the degree of social and civil destruction would seem to have been less profound and long-lasting than in the case of communist Slovakia. The 'totalitarian' character of the communist regime in the political, economic, and socio-psychological spheres has had consequences that are still visible in Slovak society today. The weakness of small businesses, the atmosphere of passivity, the acceptance or fear of authority, the relative lack of socio-cultural differentiation in mainstream society – all of these may be consequences of the recent totalitarian experience. But at the same time, some of the causes of the weakness of Slovak civil society and political culture may have to be traced further back in history, to events before the recent period of communism.

---

[7] Jacques Georgel, *Le Salazarisme: Histoire et Bilan 1926-1974* (Paris, 1981), p. 302, quoted in Birmingham, *A Concise History of Portugal*, p. 164.

[8] Birmingham, *A Concise History of Portugal*, p. 168.

It is true that in Portugal there is a considerable degree of civic and political indifference or abstention in elections as well, as has been shown in a recent publication. Yet in the elections for the European Parliament in 2004 more than 60 per cent of the Portuguese electorate went to the polls,[9] as against less than 20 per cent in Slovakia. Indeed, Slovakia has the questionable honour of showing the lowest percentage of active voters in the European Election of all the EU member states both in 2004 and in 2009. In Portugal the level of civil apathy, political indifference, and 'social amorphism' (lack of expression and differentiation) is not as high as in Slovakia, and the average observer would probably feel that Portuguese society is more vibrant than its Slovak counterpart, where spontaneous civil initiatives are rare. Slovak society and the Slovak people thus appear to be more severely affected by their historical experience than the Portuguese, even though in Portugal institutional rigidities and a degree of social conservatism may be proof of the lasting effects of the long period of dictatorship or earlier historical experiences.

Slovakia has to contend not only with the legacy of communist totalitarianism, but also with problems of long-unfulfilled national aspirations, internal divisions over the meaning of national identity, and traditional tensions over the 'Hungarian issue'. In Portugal, it is true, old divisions of liberal progressivism versus Catholic or national conservatism have persisted as well, continuing to be a factor in culture and politics even if they were toned down in recent decades. At the same time, a more inclusive sense of Portuguese nationalism is occasionally asserted as a result of rivalry or antagonism in respect of neighbouring Spain. But in Slovakia national feelings of an older ethno-cultural type are kept alive much more strongly than could ever be the case in Portugal because of the historic problematic of the relationship between the Slovaks and their 'arch-enemy' Hungary, which is still mistrusted. It sometimes seems as if this sense of insecurity produces a psychological instability that is further intensified by internal divisions among the Slovaks themselves about the nature of Slovak identity. Those who

---

[9] António Reis (ed.), *A Portrait of Portugal: Facts and Events* (Lisbon, 2007), pp. 31-3.

claim they are the only true Slovak nationalists and protectors of the nation tend to suggest that other political groups are not sufficiently patriotic or alert over the Hungarian 'threat'. Thus, both the domestic political landscape and the problem of Slovak-Hungarian relations are factors slowing down the development of a more mature political culture and civil society in Slovakia. The 'national issue' in Slovakia, the legacy of communist totalitarianism, but also forms of 'social primitivism' — manifesting themselves in a weak civil society, immature political culture, and clientelist and kleptocratic tendencies — are a fatal combination making the consolidation of a more civil and truly patriotic democracy and also a more stable party-political spectrum unusually difficult.[10] In comparison, the post-dictatorial case of Portugal appears to be an easier problem to address in political, social, psychological, and multi-ethnic terms. An important aspect of the broader issue is the position of ethnic, national, and cultural minorities in both countries.

Ethno-national and 'multicultural' problems compared

Slovakia has two relatively large minority groups within its borders, whose status and position is sometimes seen as 'problematical'. The first is the Hungarian (Magyar) minority that represents about 10 per cent of Slovakia's total population of approximately 5.5 million; the historical background and political ramifications of this question have already been discussed. The second minority issue in Slovakia, but one of a rather different kind, is that of the Roma, a population group of almost the same size as the Hungarians (the precise number of Roma is not known); it constitutes a problem of social integration but arguably also of cultural difference. Portugal, indeed, has a Roma minority as well, and a comparative analysis of the position of the Slovak and the Portuguese Roma could be useful to improve our understanding of the issue.

---

[10] See for these problems Pieter van Duin and Zuzana Poláčková, 'Distant Land in the Heart of Europe: Problems of Political Culture in Slovakia', *Central European Political Science Review*, Vol. 2, No. 6 (Winter 2001), pp. 138-50.

The size of the Portuguese Roma population is estimated at 25,000 to 30,000 people, less than one tenth of the Roma population of Slovakia, and while the latter represents 5-10 per cent of the total Slovak population, the Portuguese Roma are an insignificant fraction of the Portuguese population of some 10 million. Even so, the Roma are seen in Portugal as a significant or problematical phenomenon, as an 'ethnic minority' which is 'socially and culturally different and disadvantaged'.[11] This way of defining the situation refers to an aspect of ethno-cultural difference (arguably a problem under some circumstances) on the one hand, and an aspect of social marginalisation (a problem when the aim is to integrate people into the labour market or even mainstream society) on the other. However, in Portugal the major issue in the field of ethnic minorities is the position of the substantial and growing group of people from the former Portuguese colonies in Africa and, to a lesser degree, from Brazil and Asia. Some of these immigrants are well integrated or have Portuguese citizenship, but a larger number constitute a distinct and somewhat marginal population consisting of diverse cultural, ethnic, and social groups. Even for Portugal with its longstanding non-European contacts, mass immigration from outside Europe is a relatively new phenomenon. But before we look into this question in greater detail, a word must be said about another type of mass migration, namely emigration and return migration of Portuguese and Slovaks themselves. This tells us something about Portuguese and Slovak attitudes in terms of maintaining national identity.

In contrast to the recent mass immigration, large-scale emigration of impoverished Portuguese is not a new phenomenon. It already started in the sixteenth century, continued through the eighteenth century and after, and only recently began to slow down as a result of rising prosperity levels following Portugal's democratic revolution and the country's access to the EU. Especially the late nineteenth and early twentieth century was a unique phase of European mass emigration, which also included large numbers of

---

[11] See Reis, *A Portrait of Portugal: Facts and Events*, pp. 58-65 on immigrants and minorities.

Portuguese who continued to immigrate to Brazil, with North America being a second important destination. Later, after World War II, a remarkable number of Portuguese moved to European countries like France, Germany, and Switzerland. However, during the second and third quarters of the twentieth century a possibly even larger number went to the Portuguese colonies in Africa, especially Angola. The Portuguese Diaspora became an international 'Lusophone' community that continued to cultivate Portuguese culture and national identity. In this respect, the nineteenth- and twentieth-century history and collective behaviour of the Slovaks was very similar. They, too, tended to take their national culture abroad and to stay interested in developments at home. Today, the Slovaks still have a 'Slovak World Congress' which regularly meets as a platform discussing Slovak issues and interests. Both the Slovaks and the Portuguese, in other words, displayed a tendency of 'cultural persistence', of preserving their national culture, language, and identity. This sometimes slowed down the other 'natural' migrant tendency of assimilating into the new but alien environment of Canada and the United States, or indeed of other European countries after 1945.[12] As a result, many Portuguese and Slovaks returned to their homeland at old age in the manner of *Gastarbeiter*. When the Portuguese colonies in Africa became independent in 1974-75, a wave of return migration followed. More than half a million Portuguese returned to Portugal from Angola, Mozambique, and other former Portuguese African territories; another substantial number moved to South Africa.

Thus, both Portugal and Slovakia experienced mass emigration (and emigrant cultural persistence) but only Portugal, not Slovakia, was confronted with the new phenomenon of mass

---

[12] See for Portuguese emigration and cultural persistence M.B. Rocha-Trindade, 'A emigração, motor de relações culturais', in H. Fernandes, I. Castro Henriques, J. da Silva Horta, and S. Campos Matos (eds.), *Nação e Identidades. Portugal, os Portugueses e os Outros* (Lisbon, 2009), pp. 287-304; also Marion Kaplan, *The Portuguese. The Land and its People* (Harmondsworth, 1991), p. 164 where a figure of 4 million Portuguese abroad is mentioned, including large numbers in South Africa, Venezuela, Canada, and the United States. See Reis, *A Portrait of Portugal: Facts and Events*, p. 60 for the massive wave of Portuguese returnees from Africa in the 1970s.

immigration of non-Europeans to Europe during the second half of the twentieth century. For Portugal, which first had to absorb the white African returnees in the 1970s, this development only seriously started in the 1980s with the arrival of growing numbers of black Africans from former Portuguese colonies and economic immigrants from Brazil. By 1996 there were at least 110,000 Africans in Portugal, including people from Cape Verde, Angola, and Guinea-Bissau. In addition, there were more than 20,000 Brazilians, albeit with a much higher proportion of skilled and qualified people than among the Africans. The number of immigrants continued to grow and by 2001-2 some 170,000 immigrant workers had been legalised. After 2000 large numbers of East Europeans began to migrate to Portugal as well, and soon there were more than 100,000 of them in the country, the largest group being Ukrainians. There were also smaller numbers of foreign Chinese, Indians, and other Asians, some 25,000 of them by 2006. A separate group are the more than 30,000 Indians from the former Portuguese colony of Goa, all of whom are Portuguese citizens. In 2006 there were altogether some 500,000 foreigners in Portugal, about 5 per cent of the Portuguese population, but the real number is even higher because the official figures do not include the category of illegal immigrants.

The cultural and ethnic profile of the non-Portuguese population is very diverse. Half or more of all foreigners are Portuguese-speakers, including some 100,000 Brazilians and more than 150,000 Africans from Cape Verde, Angola, Guinea-Bissau, and other African countries; of the non-Portuguese-speakers, especially significant are the large numbers of Ukrainians, Romanians, and Moldavians. The number of Africans is actually larger than their share of the 'foreign' population suggests, because 30,000 to 40,000 of them recently acquired Portuguese citizenship; the total number of people of African descent would therefore seem to be some 200,000. The group of 'Afro-Portuguese' citizens is said to have a sociocultural profile distinguishing them from more recently arrived African migrant labourers, being 'relatively well integrated and culturally similar' to the Portuguese. Insofar as these Portuguese citizens of African descent are seen as an 'ethnic minority' — and of course they are visible as a 'racial' group—they are only one minority among many.[13]

Portugal, thus, contains a number of ethnic, social, cultural, religious, and linguistic minorities who are not foreigners but Portuguese citizens. This shows that Portugal is a multicultural country not only in terms of receiving large numbers of immigrants, but also in terms of diversity, of counting cultural and other minorities among its citizenry. The Roma minority has already been mentioned as a special case, and it may be added that even the younger generation of Roma (like in Slovakia) remain stuck in a socially marginal position, being worse off in educational and professional terms than even the lower class of Africans. The other extreme, positively speaking, are the Portuguese Indians, of whom there are more than 30,000 and who are not different from the Portuguese mainstream population in social and economic terms. Many of them are owners of small businesses and belong to the middle and lower middle classes, while the majority of their children have actually higher than average school results and often enter the commercial sector of the economy. But at the same time they tend to be different in religious or cultural terms and to some extent in linguistic terms as well, while mainly socialising amongst themselves.

In this respect, the position and pattern of behaviour of the population of African descent is quite different, above all of those Africans who are fully integrated and who are Portuguese citizens, but also of those who are more recent immigrants. Even the latter are usually Portuguese-speakers and the majority are Christians, although there is a Muslim minority from Guinea-Bissau and a tendency among some of the West Africans to retain the use of African Creole languages. While the Africans are usually not much different from mainstream Portuguese society in cultural and linguistic terms, they are more different in terms of economic and social position, and there is an element of 'subcultural' difference as far as patterns of sociability and social and cultural behaviour are concerned. Nevertheless, the trend seems to be that the second generation of Africans becomes more socially integrated through

---

[13] Reis, *A Portrait of Portugal: Facts and Events*, pp. 58-65.

educational mobility, even if a certain number of young Africans drop out of school and thus block their chances of further social mobility and integration.

As a rule, in terms of general sociability, the African population, both the Portuguese citizens among them and the 'foreigners', tend to interact with the mainstream society in a greater number of ways than both the socially marginal and isolated Roma and the culturally somewhat marginal but economically successful Indians. This complex of groups and factors makes for interesting comparative research material, for example with regard to social policy. Indeed, as far as the growing African population is concerned, it has been observed that their chances of further integration in Portuguese society are relatively good, but also that various consciously implemented social policies and encouragement of local political participation are indispensable additional instruments to achieve this aim, as is the willingness of society as a whole to grant Portuguese citizenship to a larger number of people, notably to the children of immigrants. Finally, the large group of recently arrived Eastern Europeans in Portugal seems to be perceived by the Portuguese as possessing a large number of contrasting social and cultural characteristics compared with themselves. This is especially the case with regard to social position and social behaviour as well as language and religion, but less so in terms of education or residence.[14] What this means for the further development of the relations between the Portuguese and the Eastern European immigrants remains as yet unclear. However, the question is of importance because of the possible existence or emergence of stereotypes of 'Eastern Europeans' in Western and Southern European countries like Portugal.

Conclusions

If Portugal is mainly affected by the presence of ethnic minorities resulting from the relatively new phenomenon of mass immigration, Slovakia is above all trying to deal with its old issue of defining

---

[14] Ibid.

the position of the Hungarian minority and its other problem of trying to integrate its substantial Roma population. The difference between these two national constellations may seem wide, but in many ways they are problems that share a number of social and political features and are common to Europe as a whole. The question of multicultural diversity in Europe's individual 'nation-states', for the better or the worse, is increasingly becoming an issue that is part of Europe itself as an emerging unity and as a platform of transnational and multicultural communication and problem-solving.[15] Europe has to learn to live with cultural, ethnic, and national diversity, and in fact the continent itself is a perfect historical and present-day example of this diversity, a truth that was pushed somewhat into the background in the age of nationalism and the rising national state in the nineteenth and early twentieth century. Also, the consciousness of belonging to Europe has been growing in recent decades, and both Slovakia and Portugal have their own history in this respect.[16]

In many ways, Portugal and Slovakia are comparable cases of somewhat special nations in Europe. Both countries were 'peripheral' in Europe not only in a geographic sense but also in terms of twentieth-century political history in general and their rather problematical development of democratic political culture and civil society in particular. Portugal is one of the oldest kingdoms in Europe dating back to the early twelfth century, but a more modern national identity and national consciousness only emerged in the seventeenth century during the struggle for independence from Spain, and even then it did not yet include an awareness of the need for social and political modernisation. Slovakia was part of an even older entity, the Hungarian Kingdom, and the Slovak people are arguably an old ethnic and cultural nation even if they were barred from expressing this in a 'political' sense. Their own state, therefore,

---

[15] See for a Spanish or 'Iberian' perspective on this M. Samaniego Boneu, 'Nación y multiculturalismo', in Fernandes et al. (eds.), *Nação e Identidades. Portugal, os Portugueses e os Outros*, pp. 413-24.

[16] See for the Portuguese case M.M. Tavares Ribeiro, 'Relações Portugal-Europa (séculos XIX e XX)', in Fernandes et al. (eds.), *Nação e Identidades. Portugal, os Portugueses e os Outros*, pp. 395-411.

must be counted among the most recent creations of modern European history. In their own way, each of the two countries found itself in a somewhat isolated and peripheral position vis-á-vis Europe, even Portugal with its spectacular but rather self-contained colonial adventures. Portugal's relative isolation further increased at a later stage of European history and the country missed several opportunities to develop and modernise itself. The story of Slovakia, which also seemed condemned to relative stagnation between the sixteenth and twentieth centuries, is similar in a number of ways. By the twentieth century both countries had to pay the price for this and struggled to make up for their backwardness in political, economic, and cultural terms. Nowadays it would seem that the Portuguese as well as the Slovaks are keenly aware of the importance of the European framework for succeeding in this effort.

2. Gender, power, and social disciplining: comparative observations on the position of women in early modern Slovakia and the Iberian Peninsula

This essay proffers a comparative analysis of the position of women in early modern Slovakia (Upper Hungary) and the Iberian Peninsula, focusing on 'positive' as well as 'negative' aspects of their experiences. It is argued that in the fields of culture, religion, and education progress was made in terms of rising educational and social opportunities for at least some groups of women in regions like Slovakia and Portugal. The same held true, as far as social attitudes were concerned among parts of the male population. But probably the most depressing — though also contradictory — feature of the early modern era was the question of witchcraft accusations, of which large numbers of women became victims. The 'witch-craze' can be seen in the context of a desire on the part of both clerical and secular authorities to impose greater social discipline on local communities, although the 'demonological' beliefs of many people involved should not be underestimated. Indeed, it would seem that even some of the female victims themselves believed that they actually disposed of supernatural powers and could influence certain conditions and affairs in their own communities.

The early modern period — roughly the era between the fifteenth and the eighteenth centuries — was a time when some notable changes occurred in the cultures and societies of different parts of Europe, including the Iberian Peninsula and the region of East-Central Europe. These changes also influenced the position of women in the multinational Kingdom of Hungary, within which Slovakia was known as 'Upper Hungary', as well as in Portugal and Spain. With some of these changes bringing a (potential) improvement for some groups of women and other changes causing a deterioration of their social position or even a threat to their life, the general trend appears ambivalent and justifies a closer look at some of the relevant details.

Religion, culture, and education

An example of a change for the better in the position of women in some parts of East-Central Europe was the (temporary) victory of the Protestant Reformation, to which a majority of Slovaks, Magyars (ethnic Hungarians) and other ethnic groups in multinational Hungary showed allegiance during most of the sixteenth and seventeenth centuries. The dominance of the Lutheran Church among the Slovaks until the late seventeenth century meant, among other things, that a new social and cultural stratum came into being: an intellectual or at least half-intellectual middle-class group of educated pastors and teachers and their families, which in a number of ways began to dominate life in the local Slovak Protestant communities. Once Protestant preachers and local pastors were allowed to marry and thus form families and tighter social networks, it became easier for religious and secular knowledge and for new ideas and new social attitudes to spread amongst larger and more stable groups of people, including women. The Reformation also gave rise to a much denser and wider network of elementary and secondary schools than had ever existed before. In addition, in the sixteenth and seventeenth centuries elementary schools for girls were not uncommon in many towns of Slovakia, and it seems that in western Slovakia almost every village had an elementary school by 1600, to some of which girls were admitted as well.[17] Thus, a growing number of girls and young women began to enjoy improved educational opportunities, which sometimes also meant better social and economic opportunities.

But remarkably, even among the Catholic population of Upper Hungary, whose size began to grow again as the Counter-Reformation in the region became more successful after the mid-seventeenth century, educational and social opportunities for some women began to improve by the latter part of the century. The cultural and intellectual leaders of the Counter-Reformation in Hungary understood very well that education was a major factor in the

---

[17] Viliam Čičaj, 'The period of religious disturbances in Slovakia', in Mikuláš Teich, Dušan Kováč, and Martin D. Brown (eds.), *Slovakia in History* (Cambridge, 2011), pp. 71-86, here p. 82.

struggle against the Protestants, who had to be fought with their own weapons, and that the education of women should be part of the Catholic religious revival and cultural programme as well. Thus, a situation of inter-confessional rivalry and long-term religious conflict could actually have some positive consequences for women, if only because of the strategic and pragmatic need to improve one's own position in local communities vis-à-vis the religious adversary in terms of 'ideological', social, and educational strength.

Of special interest in this connection was the introduction of the Catholic religious order of the Ursulines in Upper Hungary. This order of nuns had been founded in Italy in the sixteenth century, with a strong focus on education. In 1676 the first Ursuline cloister and school in Upper Hungary were opened in Bratislava (Pressburg), followed later by establishments in Trnava and Košice. The principal objective of the Ursuline nuns was women's education in various fields rather than monastic life, and already during the first year of the Bratislava school seventeen schoolgirls residing in the cloister itself and no less than one hundred from outside (presumably most of them from the city) were admitted to educational classes. They were taught decency and good behaviour and of course religious knowledge, but remarkably enough their curriculum also included learning to read and write Latin, something that was by no means the rule in an age when women were usually prevented from learning this language of universal education. Apart from that, the girls in the Ursuline schools were taught all kinds of useful manual labour to help them — many being from poor families — to find work and earn a decent living. Remarkable, too, were the pedagogic ideas of the Ursulines. The methods of teaching were adapted to the pupils' level of understanding but it was also stressed in the Ursuline school regulations that the girls should get tasks that would encourage their independent thinking.[18] Ursuline

---

[18] Peter Kónya (ed.), *Pramene k dejinám Slovenska a Slovákov, VII, 2: Turci v Uhorsku II. Život v Uhorskom kráľovstve počas tureckých vojen a protihabsburských povstaní od snemu v roku 1608 do satmárskeho mieru* [Sources on the history of Slovakia and the Slovaks, Vol. VII, Part 2: The Turks in Hungary, II. Life in the Hungarian

education may have helped not only to raise the social and intellectual level of many hundreds or even thousands of girls in Slovakia, but also to enable a fairly large number to find employment of a better type than would otherwise have been available to them. It may be surmised that many of the Ursuline-educated girls entered a more attractive part of the urban labour market as domestic servants and in other service occupations. This may have meant, to some extent, an improvement in the quality of their life.

On a higher social and cultural level, a growing number of women began to benefit from the new educational opportunities as well. This applied, for example, to some aristocratic women, both Protestant and Catholic, but also to women that belonged to the new educated middle-class milieu of the Lutheran and Calvinist communities in Slovakia and other parts of Hungary. Within these Protestant communities some educated women played a socially prominent role, even though it is difficult to establish how many women in the Slovak Lutheran community, for example, were in a position to express themselves more 'independently' in a cultural or intellectual way. Activities in the field of literature or autonomous religious expression would be examples of this. Clearly, more research needs to be done on this question as well as on that of the position of educated women belonging to the Upper Hungarian aristocracy or the Slovak-speaking lower nobility.

It is remarkable that with regard to Portugal, a country that is not usually associated with enlightened trends after its golden age in the fifteenth and sixteenth centuries, there are some interesting data on the participation of women in the field of literature shortly after 1700. During the first half of the eighteenth century, indeed, the number of literate women in Portugal apparently grew; but a substantial proportion, probably even the great majority, of this special group of women were Catholic nuns. Between 1701 and 1750 some 134 Portuguese literary works by female religious authors were published, a sign that in some ways the 'Enlightenment' (in the sense of creating a larger educated and literary public) had

---

Kingdom during the Turkish wars and the anti-Habsburg uprisings from the Diet of 1608 to the Peace of Szatmár] (Bratislava, 2006), pp. 238-9.

begun to influence Portugal, although we must be cautious not to jump to conclusions. This new trend was in any case remarkable enough for some men to explicitly comment on it, either negatively or positively. A case in point is Francisco Xavier de Oliveira, known as a rather eccentric and progressive figure, who compared these learned women to 'circus horses'. He may have objected to the predominantly religious orientation of their literary products, but his comment can also be seen as an expression of misogynistic tendencies. The Portuguese theologian Luís António Verney, on the other hand, considered it irrational to suppose that women were intellectually inferior to men, and believed that educating women would benefit the whole of society.[19] Thus, it seemed that there was a variety of opinions on the subject, with a theologian being more 'progressive' than an eighteenth-century individualist of sorts. In addition to these exceptional examples, there were many more men with more enlightened and tolerant views about the position of women in society, feeling the need to promote their educational, cultural, and intellectual advancement. It would be interesting to know more about what women thought or said about this controversial question themselves, on the Iberian Peninsula, in Central Europe, or elsewhere.

Perhaps most remarkable, to conclude our observations on this aspect, were the views of the enlightened Spanish Benedictine theologian Benito Feijóo, who wrote an essay in 1737 entitled 'In Defence of Women' (*Defensa de las mujeres*). There, Feijóo spoke without reservation of the aptitude of women 'for all kinds of sciences and higher knowledge', and of their political and economic prudence. He said that the usual arguments used against women in this regard were made by superficial men, and that 'one cannot infer from the fact that women do not know how to do something the idea that they have no talent for it.'[20] This observation by Feijóo can be seen as the archetypical enlightened viewpoint on the subject,

---

[19] A.R. Disney, A history of Portugal and the Portuguese Empire from beginnings to 1807, Vol. I: Portugal (Cambridge, 2009), pp. 275-6.

[20] Jon Cowans (ed.), *Early Modern Spain: A Documentary History* (Philadelphia, 2003), pp. 210-11.

which was destined to become more influential on the Iberian Peninsula in spite of all the existing obstacles.

Contours and background of the witch-craze

If in the fields of education and 'high culture' some progress was made during the early modern era in terms of social attitudes towards the position of women, there were other social realities in respect of which their position was less promising to say the least. There were threats on both the 'intellectual' and the societal level, and arguably most significant in this connection was the rise of accusations of sorcery and witchcraft practices levelled against relatively large numbers of women in various parts of Europe, both Catholic and Protestant. Historians of the 'witch-craze' have estimated that about 80% of the victims of witchcraft accusations and of the interrogations, torture, and executions that often followed were women, only 20% being men.[21]

It was partly an extreme manifestation of the 'traditional' stigmatisation of those women who in one way or another did not entirely conform to the conventional, presumably 'normal' pattern of life in the average village or town community or who occupied a somewhat marginal or isolated position within the community, often as elderly women and widows (in the words of H.R. Trevor-Roper, 'the ordinary victims of village hatred').[22] But younger women also could become victims of witchcraft accusations. Indeed, it can be argued that the evidence on witchcraft trials in a region like Upper Hungary can be used to reconstruct the existence of internal tensions in many village and town communities, including rivalry and open conflicts between individual women or groups of women. It is these conflicts that actually formed the background to at least a part of the documented witch-craze cases and to the

---

[21] Jean-Michel Sallmann, "Witches" (Translated from the French by Arthur Goldhammer), in Natalie Zemon Davis and Arlette Farge (eds.), *A History of Women in the West, Vol. III: Renaissance and Enlightenment Paradoxes* (Cambridge, Mass. and London, 1993), pp. 444-57, here p. 445.

[22] H.R. Trevor-Roper, *The European Witch-Craze of the 16th and 17th Centuries* (Harmondsworth, 1969), p. 120.

remarkable phenomenon that some women seem to have been genuinely convinced of wielding supernatural powers. In other words, witchcraft accusations were not always 'imposed from above', but sometimes also emerged 'from below'.

Historians of the witch-craze have shown that, especially in mountainous and relatively isolated regions and communities, suspicions of heresy, heretical devil-worship, or various forms of sorcery and witchcraft were often prevalent among local parish priests and other customary representatives of religious orthodoxy. In regions which historically had been the core of the medieval Christian social and cultural system this was the case to a lesser extent. Famous, for example, are the studies by Julio Caro Baroja on witchcraft in the Basque Country, and other historians have supported the 'mountain thesis' as well.[23] But this 'macro-sociological' feature cannot entirely explain all local peculiarities of the witch-craze or the social subtleties of local communities; even less the historical fact that the hysteria began to influence almost the whole of Europe from the fifteenth century onwards. Incidentally, the world of Eastern Orthodox Christianity was apparently much less affected, possibly because of the non-existence of an internal 'Reformation problem' or other religious and intellectual tensions in Eastern and South-Eastern Europe.

Indeed, quite apart from any sociological dimension, there emerged a new 'demonology' within the world of the Western Church, a kind of quasi-theological and quasi-scientific belief in the existence of witchcraft as a pact with the devil more or less consciously entered into by certain individuals or groups of people. This 'systematisation' of witchcraft theory gained traction after the publication of the *Malleus Maleficarum* ('Hammer of Witches') in 1486. The spread of the new demonology among learned men was followed by the outside intervention into the day-to-day affairs of local communities, although some urban and even rural communities may already have been influenced in a more gradual way by the new ideas on witchcraft. Examples of institutions intervening in

---

[23] Julio Caro Baroja, *The World of the Witches*, translated from the Spanish by Nigel Glendinning (London, 2001); Trevor-Roper, *The European Witch-Craze*.

local witchcraft scandals and in some cases causing or at least exacerbating them were the Inquisition in Spain and Portugal and the political and judicial authorities on the county level in Upper Hungary. In some cases, this introduced increased superstitious suspicion or quasi-theological paranoia into the arena of the local community with its often long-standing social tensions. Local conflicts began to be influenced by notions that were partly derived from outside, but which in some cases had also been cultivated within the local community itself. The traditional nature of local social conflicts remained in many cases the background to what was happening in a village or town community. However, old tensions, prejudices, and superstitions could now become exacerbated by a new kind of alertness regarding alleged sorcery and witchcraft practices.

In a religiously divided society like seventeenth-century Slovakia, the phenomenon of witchcraft hysteria may have been reinforced by the attempts of both Protestants and Catholics to 'purify' their own communities and to root out heretics and other non-conformists. Indeed, both confessional communities were affected by the witch-craze, the Protestants no less than the Catholics. In the background there were endeavours in many rural and urban communities to strengthen social control and moral discipline. All kinds of fears, uncertainties, and conflicts played a role in daily life, and the local priest or pastor could try to strengthen his authority by responding to witchcraft accusations, sometimes supported by the higher Church institutions. Religious conflicts in the wider society, combined with the violence of the wars against the Ottoman Empire, social upheaval caused by peasant unrest, and other dislocating factors, partly undermined the existing social control mechanisms, which were normally upheld by the landlords and the local and county authorities. The resulting sense of insecurity could lead to increased aggression against those who were suspected of practising harmful forms of magic, sorcery, or witchcraft—matters that previously might have been tolerated as features of village tradition and superstitious folklore, but now no longer were permitted by the higher authorities or indeed by some members of the local community itself.

At the same time, and perhaps even more important, some women living in stressful circumstances might be tempted to use the (old or new) idea of manipulative witchcraft practices to regain a sense of power over their own lives and the lives of others or even of the local community as such. In increasingly unstable, chaotic, and unpredictable conditions, women could come to see themselves as the prime protectors of their families and friends, and as special individuals with the ability to influence their fate and increase their own importance in local society. But precisely this could also be seen by others as a threat to the normal functioning *of* and the 'natural order' *in* society, especially when social and political conditions seemed to be deteriorating.

Additionally, the self-conscious acting out of 'witch identity' in Upper Hungary came against the backdrop of the unsettled state of war-marked seventeenth-century Hungary (divided between Habsburg, Ottoman, and Transylvanian territories), which caused abnormal demographic changes in the sex ratio in many regions and local communities. Large numbers of men were killed in the Turkish wars, and most men died earlier than women anyway, causing the well-known early modern phenomenon of large-scale female widowhood. At the same time, there were numerous garrisons of foreign soldiers in the towns and fortifications along the Hungarian-Ottoman frontier. This may have tempted poor single women into prostitution, a practice that some local authorities tried to suppress while it apparently was tolerated by others. In other cases, the surplus of women over men in communities affected by endemic violence and war could enhance the freedom of individual women or lead to competition between them for the limited number of men and potential husbands available.

All these social and demographic problems were bound to complicate the aim of maintaining a 'decent' moral and social order as desired by the local Protestant, Catholic, or secular authorities.

Problems of social disciplining, community conflict, and witchcraft

A few examples of 'immoral' behaviour in Upper Hungary throw light on some of these seventeenth-century problems and on the links between a more general social crisis and the phenomenon of witchcraft. In 1676 a man with two wives and one mistress was sentenced to death in the county of Spiš in eastern Slovakia. His apparently somewhat exhibitionist style of practising polygamy was obviously too much for the irritated local authorities. In 1695, in the town of Prešov in the adjoining county of Šariš, two women accused of prostitution were tried and found guilty for reportedly having respected 'neither God nor human law'. They had come to Prešov from a nearby village to prostitute themselves for soldiers of the winter garrison. The local judge wanted to set an example and demanded that they be burnt at the stake, but one of the women was married and said they had been forced to come and see the soldiers by the mayor of their home village. However, the mayor insisted that they had gone to Prešov voluntarily and had demanded money from the soldiers with whom they fornicated. Finally, it was decided that the two women should have a cross branded on their back and be expelled from the county for the rest of their life. If they returned they were to be executed.[24] Further below we will see how particular social problems could be related to the witch-craze in Upper Hungary, but first we will take a look at the Iberian Peninsula.

In Portugal and Spain, with many men being away in the colonies, similar problems of social disorder and instability may have existed and also similar social factors causing tensions in local communities including witchcraft accusations, some of which the local authorities or outside institutions considered important enough to investigate. If in some ways there were different cultural, religious, and political realities, in other ways the situation in Slovakia and conditions in certain parts of the Iberian Peninsula were

---

[24] Kónya (ed.), *Pramene k dejinám Slovenska a Slovákov, VII, 2: Turci v Uhorsku II*, pp. 368-9.

comparable. In sixteenth- and seventeenth-century Spain the Inquisition was less concerned with detecting witchcraft practices than with the persecution of *conversos* (converted but mistrusted Jews) and *moriscos* (Muslims). But its role in helping to control and discipline the old Christian population increased during the seventeenth century as well. This opened the way to mutual denunciations in local communities with their manifold personal and group conflicts, and indeed, much of the surviving judicial evidence consists of what some people said about others. In the sexual sphere, where rural society was often less disciplined than urban society, the challenge seems to have been imposing urban rigour on rural laxity. Apparently, both women and men were frequent bigamists in rural seventeenth-century Spain. But besides addressing problems of social discipline, the Spanish Inquisition's concern with suppressing popular superstitions and magical and witchcraft practices markedly increased as well. As we have seen, the new 'demonological interpretation' of these traditional phenomena had already emerged at an earlier stage. With the decline in the number of cases of pure religious heresy in the seventeenth century—long seen as a bigger issue than witchcraft—increasing attention was now being paid to more eccentric problems.

Witchcraft was presumed to exist primarily in Spain's northern provinces, notably Navarra, the Basque Country, Asturias, and Galicia—isolated regions which also had an old, if ill-defined, 'heresy' problem. Perhaps this confirms the observation made by some historians that heresy and witchcraft were linked, at least in the eyes of the Inquisition persecutors. At the same time, the Spanish sceptics doubting the existence of witchcraft were relatively influential, which in fact saved the country from a mass witch-hysteria. Like other sceptics elsewhere in Europe, they often argued that people accused of, or even admitting to have engaged in sorcery or devil-worship, were actually suffering from 'melancholy', madness, or other delusions. Some Inquisition sceptics even dared to express their conviction that many witchcraft tales were pure fantasy, produced by the accused and victims themselves if not by the inquisitors. Trevor-Roper speaks in this connection of the 'mental rubbish of peasant credulity and feminine hysteria', which nonetheless could be used as material from which a quasi-learned demonology was constructed or which could be employed as a form of self-aggrandisement by some of the accused, who were suffering from 'melancholy'. In addition, while the degree of social control in the more isolated countryside was always limited, people could try to use the Inquisition or other outside institutions as a tool in their conflicts. One such strategy was to accuse other members of the community of being 'bad Christians' or other vices in order to harm rivals and enemies. Interestingly, to prevent this problem Spanish parish priests would urge their flock not to engage in 'telling things about each other' when the inquisitors came to visit their village.[25] Problems of attempted social disciplining and fear of witchcraft could have unexpected effects.

The importance of the micro-sociological aspect, i.e. of local conditions and social conflict involving women, can be illuminated even better by evidence on witch-trials in seventeenth-century Slovakia. In Hungary and the ethnic Slovak regions the witch-craze affected the aristocracy, the towns, the rural population, and the clergy. The notorious case of the sadistic aristocratic woman Erzsébet Báthory, who allegedly was involved in torturing and killing a large number of young women over the course of several years until she was detained in 1610, was linked to sorcery and witchcraft, too. She was said, among other things, to have practised witchcraft and acts of poisoning with the help of a well-known 'witch' from the town of Myjava in west Slovakia who would bake 'magic bread' to help kill Báthory's enemies. Around 1600 it was apparently believed that many noble ladies were trying to get magic cakes from witches and similar evil things, which may have been the expression of a double fear among the people: on the one hand fear of the rural dominant class and on the other of the practices of putative local witches. It was claimed that the Myjava witch would pray to God or to a demon or devil to give health to those she wanted to protect but to send diabolical cats 'to eat the hearts' of her enemies. Even a Slovak Lutheran pastor, who gave evidence during the

---

[25] Henry Kamen, *The Spanish Inquisition: An Historical Revision* (London, 2000), pp. 260-82; Trevor-Roper, *The European Witch-Craze*, pp. 41, 58.

investigations into the Báthory affair, warned of the evil influence of witches and expressed his fear of cats and dogs that had been bewitched by the devil and tried to harm people, including himself.[26] In insecure social situations such as those in seventeenth-century Slovakia the idea of witchcraft, or of concluding a pact with the devil, could be used for all kinds of purposes. What was a matter of sincere belief and what was instrumental was often hard to say. But there were few people, it would seem, who did not share these beliefs, not even educated Lutheran ministers.

Around the same time, in 1602, a remarkable witch-trial was held in Bratislava. Two women from a semi-rural community on the outskirts of the city had been accused of engaging in various witchcraft practices. These were essentially understood to be devil-worshipping or concluding a pact with the devil; causing harm to others by various magical practices; night-flying and riding on a broomstick; having (sexual) intercourse with demons; and attending meetings known as the Witches' Sabbath. The women, who were interrogated under torture, eventually confessed and were burnt at the stake, but it was stressed in the judicial report that they had willingly co-operated in the investigation. This may have been closer to the truth than is usually believed by those (i.e. most of us) who understandably refuse to trust evidence obtained under pressure. Indeed, it transpires from the evidence given by the two women, even if much of it was put into their mouth by their interrogators, that they cultivated the idea of possessing and wielding magic powers. They also mentioned several other women, who they said were involved in witchcraft practices as well. The evidence gives the impression — again, quite apart from the real factor of pressure — that in Bratislava and surroundings there existed a whole 'scene', almost a 'subculture', of women who competed with each other in casting spells and trying to harm others. Whereas some of them were rivals and enemies, others were friends who collaborated in pairs or groups tried to help each other or indeed damage the life of others.

---

[26] Tony Thorne, *Countess Dracula: Life and times of Elisabeth Bathory, the Blood Countess* (London, 1997), pp. 85-111.

But while the names of several other women were mentioned by the two accused either as friendly or as enemy witches, the activities of all of them were said to include the poisoning of men (some of them being family members) as well as the bewitching of both women and men, allegedly causing severe illness or death. This form of 'criminal' activity was combined with sexual immorality. Some women were said to have an intimate relationship with a devil, demon, or evil spirit, who they said usually looked like a young man. Some of these devils had a name and all were as cold as ice. Stories like this are also known from other parts of Europe and were perhaps of a fairly standard type. Women were said to swear to their own personal devil so as to invoke his support when practising sorcery, and at least one of them could in this way 'cause storms' and 'spoil other people's fruit and wine'. One of the accused women described how her devil would come to her during the night and lay next to her while her husband was sleeping beside her as well. She added, however, that she had no intercourse with her devil, and when he told her to kill her little daughter, who was always ill, she refused to do it. She often thought of God, she said, and then the devil disappeared (here the devil seems to represent her bad conscience rather than any evil intention).

Women were also said to collect herbs 'in the name of the devil', perhaps with a view to influencing the health of other people or poisoning them. Health and food matters typically figured prominently in the stories of the accused, but other pieces of evidence are much more bizarre. Indeed, one woman was said to have 'opened a human head' (apparently of a deceased person) and thrown its contents in front of the home of the local judge in order that 'the law could not be executed anymore'. Equally macabre was the story that during a terrible storm a stillborn baby had been brought to one of the accused women with the mother asking her to bury it. Not long after, the baby's mother told her to exhume and burn it because she wanted the two of them to make 'magic grease' from the burned skeleton, which would help them in their sorcery practices and broomstick flying.

Even more significant may be the evidence relating to agricultural and household matters, particularly the bewitching of cows and milk. One of the accused described how a woman had bewitched her cows and milk as well as those of other women, adding that 'with the help of a white dog' they managed to get normal milk again. When the accused and another woman tried to engage in retaliatory sorcery with a special 'wooden stick', a creature suddenly appeared 'in the shape of a black dog', which they beat and tried to kill. They soon understood that it was the enemy witch, a woman they actually knew well and whose dough they had try to spoil by casting spells.[27]

All these details may seem pretty bizarre to us, but four-hundred years ago they probably were not. In the Bratislava witch-trial of 1602 we can discern a pattern of personal and social conflicts between rival women and between women and men. We encounter the belief that sorcery and witchcraft practices entailed the possibility of protecting oneself and harming one's enemies; furthermore some rather conventional ideas about what witches were doing, part of which may have been put into the mouth of the accused; and a context of household, food, and health matters that traditionally played a prominent role in local communities, especially among women. Some of these elements could be construed by the new type of 'demonological' witch hunters as proof of dangerous heretical activities, which might be harmful to the wider community and also to accepted religious views.

'Melancholy' and imagined power: contradictory tendencies

The often rural or semi-rural context of Slovak witch-trials and the element of rivalry and enmity between women are further illustrated by events in a village in the county of Novohrad in south-central Slovakia in 1696. Here a (probably elderly) widow, one

---

[27] Viliam Čičaj (ed.), *Pramene k dejinám Slovenska a Slovákov, VII, 1: Turci v Uhorsku I. Život v Uhorskom kráľovstve počas tureckých vojen od tragickej bitky pri Moháči až do Bratislavského snemu* [Sources on the history of Slovakia and the Slovaks, Vol. VII, Part 1: The Turks in Hungary, I. Life in the Hungarian Kingdom during the Turkish wars from the tragic Battle at Mohács to the Diet of Bratislava] (Bratislava, 2005), pp. 287-91.

Mariena Gregorová, was arrested and then imprisoned in the county's administrative centre Lučenec, following accusations of sorcery and witchcraft. The case may have been typical of village and small-town conditions where fear of, and belief in the bewitching of cattle and the casting of spells in order to harm people's health was a well-known phenomenon. A large number of witnesses were summoned to testify before the village judge, who had been instructed by the county authorities to hold a trial. From the evidence it appears that the accused was an alcoholic, probably a lonely widow, who had landed in a position of social isolation. She seems to have had frequent unpleasant exchanges with other villagers, both men and women, trying to assert herself vis-à-vis the others and demanding attention by 'proving' in unusual ways that she could actually produce first-class butter from the local cows' milk. She also claimed she could produce special grease or lard with healing qualities (we have already encountered the 'magic grease' story above). And she admitted that she used to curse people she resented, saying things that sometimes sounded pitiful or poetic but at the same time threatening, for example that 'her tears would cast a spell on them'. However, to the same people she also offered her special grease, which she said was good for their health, especially for women. On one occasion Mariena and another woman got into trouble with one another over who could make the best butter; they had started to yell calling each other 'witch' (*bosorka, striga*). According to one of the witnesses summoned before the village judge, the accused would speak of devils that would prevent other women from eating proper butter, apparently suggesting that she had contact or influence with them. Allegedly she claimed she could harm other people and their possessions, even when she was not present at the place where it happened. She also insisted that she could turn a bad cow into a good one, again suggesting she was able to practise good as well as evil magic. Perhaps most serious of all was the claim made by another witness, a widow like Mariena, who said that when her husband was still alive Mariena had appeared one day near their home declaring that he was not going to live much longer. He replied she should stop drinking, but after his death more serious conclusions may have been drawn about Mariena.[28]

Perhaps this case should be interpreted as an example of the 'melancholy' — a state of mind that some of the mentioned sceptics and more rationalist-inclined theologians in Spain ascribed to widows and other unhappy individuals who were accused of witchcraft practices. Yet, there may be more to it, even when 'melancholy' was involved as well. Alcoholism surely played a part besides social isolation and village rivalries between women. Some women competed with each other both to prove their 'natural' (domestic and economic) and their 'supernatural' abilities. The latter, perhaps, were claimed in a playful, provocative, and half-serious manner, or in a state of intoxication. But arguably in some cases they were also asserted — however mad or deluded it may seem — in a more serious vein, having the psychological function of boosting the ego and a sense of power over other people, social conditions, or even life and death. Although according to a witness Mariena Gregorová had claimed on one occasion that 'maybe all the devils had carried her' (up in the air) and although she had spoken of devils at other times as well, in her case there is little evidence of a belief in a demonological phenomenon like the Witches' Sabbath. Nevertheless, traditional superstitions had been amplified to a level where some parties involved — including the county authorities, who normally distanced themselves from petty village affairs — had begun to believe that an investigation had to be made into certain witchcraft accusations. This was socially and religiously significant. Although some of the witnesses may have 'seen' or claimed more than there really was, they may have believed what they said, and this time met with a more receptive response on the part of the outside authorities. As for the accused herself, she simply may have wanted to employ notions of sorcery to enhance her own importance in a social world in which she had little importance. The same kind of thing, and even more emphatically, can be said with regard to the Bratislava trial of 1602.

The era of the witch-craze in Hungary and Slovakia seems to have both started later and continued longer than in the more

---

[28] Kónya (ed.), *Pramene k dejinám Slovenska a Slovákov, VII, 2: Turci v Uhorsku II*, pp. 362-4.

western regions of Europe, lasting well into the eighteenth century. In 1714, for example, another trial was held in a village in southwest Slovakia in which eleven women and two men were accused of witchcraft practices. Indeed, during the first half of the eighteenth century Hungary as a whole saw the largest number of witch-trials in its history with several hundred women and a few dozen men being executed for alleged witchcraft practices and many others being tortured to extort confessions.[29]

As we have seen, the phenomenon of the witch-hysteria is complex and in some ways contradictory. While women were in many ways its principal victims, paradoxically the witch-craze could provide some of them with a sense of power, however tragic this may have been. The activities of the Inquisition in Spain and Portugal and of the secular authorities in Slovakia and Hungary were often oppressive but sometimes could also be used by some of the (potential) victims to further their own ends. Witchcraft accusations could become part of a social game, of local conflicts among women or between women and other local villagers or townsmen. Meanwhile, the persecutors or interpreters from outside could produce their own version of what was going on. These aspects are among the many contradictions and uncertainties in the history of 'witchcraft' in early modern Europe, whose culture in some ways moved towards improved social and cultural conditions but in other ways seemed to fall back into a new age of barbarism. The history of European women is one way in which these events and tendencies can be described.

---

[29] Peter Kónya (ed.), *Pramene k dejinám Slovenska a Slovákov, VIII: Nový pohľad na svet. Čas osvietenských vládcov od protihabsburských povstaní po začiatky slovenského národného obrodenia* [Sources on the history of Slovakia and the Slovaks, Vol. VIII: A new worldview. The times of the enlightened rulers from the anti-Habsburg uprisings to the beginnings of the Slovak National Awakening] (Bratislava, 2007), pp. 382-91.

3. Iberian images and personalities of the Counter-Reformation in Slavic Central Europe

This essay describes the role of 'Iberian' images and symbolisms in the Central European Counter-Reformation, in particular as incarnated in 'Hispanic' military commanders and other leading personalities, who were summoned by the Austrian Habsburgs to help suppress Protestant movements in Bohemia and Hungary in the seventeenth century. The cruel Hispanic or Iberian figure, indeed, became the symbolic image *par excellence* of intolerant Catholicism and international Counter-Reformation. In contrast to the other essays in this collection, we are dealing here with a situation of direct contact and interaction between Iberian and Slavic historical actors. However, the Habsburg authorities in Central Europe and individuals from the Spanish-ruled territories in Italy were important intermediate actors in this religious, political, and military encounter. We will pay particular attention to the Czech Lands and to Slovakia (Upper Hungary), parts of Slavic Central Europe that were deeply influenced by the sixteenth-century Reformation and the complicated conflicts resulting from it. Around 1600 both the Catholic Church in Central Europe and the Austrian Habsburg (or 'Imperial German') Army had begun to employ the services of influential Iberians to fight back against the rising power of Protestantism with its many adherents among almost all social strata in Bohemia, Hungary, and even Austria itself. Those called to come to the support of the Austrian Habsburgs were largely men with important positions in the Spanish territories in Italy, especially Naples and Milan. Strategically speaking, the mobilisation of soldiers and ideologists from these nearby Italian lands proved extremely useful in strengthening the overall efficacy of the Catholic forces in the great struggle between the Church of Rome, Vienna, and Madrid on one side, and the different Protestant groups and their secular representatives in Hungary, Bohemia, and other Habsburg lands on the other.

The challenge of Slavic and Hungarian Protestantism

The Protestant groups concerned included the Czech Utraquists (Hussites), the Czech and Moravian Brethren, the Slovak and German Lutherans, and the Hungarian (mainly Magyar) Calvinists, all of whom tried to survive in the complex multi-confessional hotchpotch of early modern East-Central Europe with its cultural and political struggles in which various factions among the nobility, townsmen, and peasantry participated. While the era of the great struggle between Reformation and Counter-Reformation in Bohemia and Moravia ended with a victory for the latter in the 1620s, in Hungary it continued during the later seventeenth and the eighteenth century even though Protestantism was seriously forced into the defensive after the 1670s. The power of resistance of Hungarian Calvinism, Lutheranism, and indeed the Protestant nobility proved more enduring than elsewhere in the Habsburg Empire.

In the Czech Lands the suppression of Protestantism after the Battle of the White Mountain in 1620 led to a state of affairs that could be described as an antagonistic situation of neutralisation and virtual annihilation of the weaker confessional party. Late Hussitism and Protestantism were practically wiped out in Bohemia and Moravia, but a large part of the population withdrew into an attitude of passive antagonism and stubborn indifference to the Catholic Church, or, in some outlying areas, 'secretive Protestantism'. The situation in Slovakia and other parts of Habsburg Hungary was rather different as Protestantism managed to survive as a minority faith with the help of autonomous church institutions, constituting at least 20% of the total population and significantly higher percentages in some individual counties. This state of affairs could be described as one of active antagonism and sustained power inequality, but to some extent was also marked by a degree of pragmatic co-existence and mutual toleration. (In the early 1780s, thanks to emperor Joseph II's enlightened toleration policy, the Hungarian and Slovak Protestant communities could even begin to flourish again.) The survival of Protestantism was especially notable on the local level in some northern and eastern Hungarian regions with either a strong Lutheran (mainly Slovak or ethnic German) or

Calvinist (mainly Magyar) tradition. It was in particular the Calvinist and Lutheran nobility—but to some extent also the Free Royal Cities with their partially surviving administrative autonomy—who acted as a social and political safeguard ensuring that Magyar, Slovak, and German Protestantism could survive in various Hungarian counties. But at the same time, Catholic overall domination and the persistent antagonism between Catholics and Protestants in Hungary as a whole remained crucial features of culture, politics, and society on the local and county level, even giving rise to different forms of written language and literature in different confessional communities within the same ethnic group.

Spanish Catholic tyranny and Italian paradoxes

It is probably true that for Protestants of all denominations in central and western Europe, Iberian, Hispanic, and Spanish-Italian personalities—even if only one among various manifestations of tyrannical Catholicism—served over a long period of time as the most typical, cruel, and abhorrent symbols and incarnations of the dominant Catholic establishment they could possibly be confronted with. The fact that some of these figures were brought to Central Europe to fight on the side of the Habsburg Counter-Reformation was telling and indeed intimidating.

In this context, the notions of 'Iberian' and 'Hispanic' have to be understood in a broad sense, i.e. as including not only the two nations of the Iberian Peninsula (as well as their colonial overseas territories) but also the Spanish-ruled territories in other parts of Europe. The latter principally included Spanish Italy, i.e. the Kingdom of Naples, Sicily, Sardinia, and the Duchy of Milan (Lombardy), as well as the Spanish Netherlands, after c1600 reduced to the southern Netherlands. Between 1580 and 1640 Portugal was part of the lands of the Spanish Crown as well so that during this 'period of darkness' for Portugal, the terms 'Hispanic' and 'Iberian' were essentially identical with Spain in the widest sense of the word. The term 'Spanish' had come to refer to what was to all intents and purposes a unique Catholic world power, branching out across Italy as well and thus bordering the territory of its Austrian

Habsburg blood brother. The historical phenomenon of Spanish Italy is more important for the fate of Central and Slavic Europe than is sometimes realised. During the period with which we are concerned — mainly the seventeenth century — imperial Spain made active use of its Italian territories to intervene in the affairs of Central Europe and prop up the political, religious, and military standing of its Austrian imperial counterpart, the dominant power in Catholic Germany and non-German East-Central Europe. It was by means of Spanish Italy and Habsburg Austria that the would-be 'Universal Catholic Empire' of Imperial Spain tried to impose its will on those parts of Central Europe, including mainly Protestant Slavic lands, where the rebellious Reformation seemed dangerously close to a victory that might still be prevented by the Iberian colossus. Thus, the Italian Peninsula played a crucial role in strengthening the Catholic forces in Central Europe.

In this connection it is interesting to look in particular at the Spanish-controlled Kingdom of Naples, at the time an important principality in Italy and one with an important function both for Spain and Austria. Naples was a territory through which the Iberian-Slavic encounter was mediated in several ways: politically, militarily, culturally, and last but not least ideologically and psychologically, i.e. in terms of images of the Catholic enemy among Protestant Slavs. The city spawned a remarkable number of prominent personalities, especially in the military sphere but also in the context of the Catholic Church, who were sent to Habsburg Hungary, Bohemia, and other parts of the Austrian Habsburg Empire to help suppress Protestant and anti-Habsburg uprisings and the general influence of Protestantism ('a-Catholicism'). These men, though often Italians, were despised by their victims and enemies as representatives of Catholic imperial Spain and instruments of the transnational Hispanic power. However, and interestingly enough, Naples not only produced some remarkable ideologists and defenders of imperial Spain but also a handful of critics of the Iberian world power. This is something we briefly have to pay attention to before moving on to events in Central Europe.

One of the great figures of early seventeenth-century Naples was the philosopher and Catholic utopian thinker Tommaso

Campanella (1568-1639), a man who gradually developed a more ambivalent and critical attitude to the Spanish Empire and its claims and ambitions. Campanella, indeed, was not only the author of a famous religious utopian work, 'The City of the Sun', but also of *De Monarchia hispanica* (1601) and later works which actually criticised the politics and cultural attitudes of the Iberian superpower. If, on the one hand, Campanella believed that a Universal Catholic Monarchy was a necessity of human (and eschatological) history and that Spain was the only Christian power able to play this role in his own life-time, he also increasingly criticised Spain for what he considered its grave shortcomings, especially its 'arrogance' and its inability to deal tactfully with the cultural differences among the peoples it had come to rule. This, of course, included the Italians in Spanish territories like Naples. Even more outspoken was a Neapolitan political philosopher of a later generation, Paolo Mattia Doria (born in 1647), who wrote a remarkable work in the second decade of the eighteenth century. In *Massime del governo spagnuolo a Napoli*, Doria described the Spanish regime in Naples — which had just come to an end in 1713 — as the expression of a culture and mentality of perverted 'honour' and self-love.[30] Thus, it would be a mistake to think that all Italians in the Spanish territories of the Italian Peninsula were uncritical followers of Spanish policies. They did however tend to subscribe to the ideology of Catholic world power and universal monarchy. It was this ideology and its practical consequences that the Protestants of Central Europe were confronted with when the Austrian Habsburgs decided to mobilise Spanish-Italian military commanders in their effort to suppress anti-Catholic and anti-Habsburg uprisings.

'Iberians' in Central Europe and their image

We do not know enough about how Protestant Czechs or Slovaks perceived the different features of the Iberian Imperial or Spanish-Italian Catholic threat, or how they looked at the deeds and

---

[30] Anthony Pagden, *Spanish Imperialism and the Political Imagination: Studies in European and Spanish-American Social and Political Theory, 1513-1830* (New Haven, 1990), Chapters 2-3.

attitudes of notorious representatives of the Hispanic Empire abroad or in their own lands. However, with regard to some spectacular events in Central Europe and the role played in them by some 'Hispanic' individuals, notably men from Spanish Naples who participated in military operations in northern Hungary, we have some concrete knowledge. We also know for sure that the conclusions drawn by individual Czech, Slovak, and Hungarian commentators about these actions were extremely damaging for the reputation and the ideological symbolism of 'Iberia' and its international representatives. The main reason for this were undoubtedly the gruesome actions of some of Greater Iberia's military representatives in the Thirty Years' War and during some of the Hungarian anti-Habsburg uprisings both before and after this war.

The 'Black Legend', i.e. the bad reputation of oppressive Spain, was actively cultivated by its enemies and undoubtedly known in Central Europe as well. In addition, Hungary and Bohemia had their own experiences, which could be added to the many events and stories making up the Hispanic reputation of violence and cruelty. Iberia's involvement in the activities of the Counter-Reformation in Central Europe was mainly the work of its representatives from Spanish Italy. An Italian historian, Claudio Donati, has produced an overview of the role of Spanish-Italian military commanders in early modern Europe in an article published in 2007.[31] This and other sources enable us to begin to understand the role of Spanish-Italian figures in the military field, as well as its scope, and its consequences. Some of the most prominent men playing a major role in military actions in Slavic Central Europe while fighting for the Austrian Habsburg ally of Imperial Spain were the following.

Giorgio Basta (1544-1607), a notorious Neapolitan military commander sent to Central Europe by the King of Spain, Philip II, was a major figure in the Austrian Habsburg war in Hungary against the Turks, but also in the struggle against the Protestants of

---

[31] Claudio Donati, 'The Profession of Arms and the Nobility in Spanish Italy', in Thomas James Dandelet and John A. Marino (eds.), *Spain in Italy: Politics, Society, and Religion 1500-1700* (Leiden, 2007), Chapter 10.

northern Hungary and Transylvania. His manner of trying to suppress Protestantism in Transylvania during the years 1601-6, in a military and political campaign against anti-Habsburg rebels, undoubtedly ensured that the Spanish and Iberian reputation of merciless antagonism towards all non-Catholics was confirmed and consolidated in Central and South-East Europe. A similar case was that of an Italian from Spanish Milan, Giovanni Giacomo da Barbiano di Belgioioso (1565-1626), one of a long series of military officers and administrators from Milan and Lombardy fighting for Spain in both the Netherlands and the Austrian Habsburg lands. Di Belgioioso was sent to Upper Hungary in 1603 and became a crucial figure in 1604 when the Protestant churches in the city of Košice were forcibly closed down as part of a campaign against the Hungarian anti-Habsburg rebels led by the Calvinist magnate Bocskai. Girolamo Caraffa (1564-1633), a Habsburg military commander from an old Neapolitan noble family, played a prominent role in the Battle of White Mountain near Prague in 1620. This event in the first phase of the Thirty Years' War (1618-1648) meant the end of Czech Protestantism and religious toleration in Bohemia, Moravia, and other territories then belonging to the Bohemian Crown. Caraffa also fought in northern Hungary against the forces of the Hungarian rebel leader Gábor Bethlen, whom he prevented from coming to the support of the Protestant army in Bohemia. Tommaso Caracciolo (1572-1631), also from the Kingdom of Naples, similarly made a military career by playing an important part in the Battle of White Mountain. Thereafter he was elevated by the Austrian Habsburg (Holy Roman) emperor Ferdinand II to the prestigious post of Master Field General in Moravia. Another member of the already mentioned Caraffa family, Antonio Caraffa (1646-1693), was destined to become the most ill-reputed and most hated figure of a later bloody phase of the Counter-Reformation in Hungary in the 1670s and 1680s. It is significant that he was introduced to the Habsburg Court in Vienna by his cousin, the Catholic cardinal Carlo Caraffa della Spina.

Within the Church hierarchy and the Habsburg army (in a wider sense), the relations between Spaniards, Neapolitans, and Austrians were close, and both Slovak Lutherans and Magyar

Calvinists were counted among their victims. Hungarian Protestants began to get a first-hand impression of the Neapolitan Kingdom when in the 1670s numbers of convicted Lutheran and Calvinist ministers were sent in chains from Bratislava to the Spanish galleys at Naples. Some of them managed to escape while others were ransomed by Protestant merchants from northern Europe or liberated by enemies of the Spaniards including the Dutch admiral De Ruyter. One of those who managed to return to Central Europe, the Slovak Lutheran minister Ján Simonides, later wrote a report of his 'adventures' and experiences, which was published in Germany and served to confirm and reinforce the evil image of the Catholic Counter-Reformation and the unique cruelty of Spain and its allies. Simonides' manuscript from 1676 became known as *Väznenie, vyslobodenie a putovanie Jána Simonidesa a jeho druha Tobiáša Masníka* ('The imprisonment, liberation, and wanderings of Ján Simonides and his companion Tobiáš Masník'), Masník being another Slovak Lutheran minister who shared the same fate as Simonides.[32] But even more notorious than this became a series of events in eastern Slovakia in the 1680s and a text which gave a graphic and shocking account of them.

Antonio Caraffa and the 'Prešov slaughterhouse'

When in the 1680s the project of trying to annihilate Protestantism in Hungary by military means reached its culmination in some parts of the country, it was Antonio Caraffa who came to the fore as General Commissary of the Habsburg Army, military governor of Upper Hungary, and royal commissioner of Transylvania. Caraffa was destined to become the most infamous Italian and Hispanic oppressor in the religious and political history of Slovakia and Habsburg Hungary. As military governor of Upper Hungary he established a reputation as an unequalled bloodhound by setting up in 1687 an illegal 'Executive Court' engaged in persecuting, torturing, and executing not only the followers of the Protestant

---

[32] Simonides' text is available in modern Slovak in the 'electronic library' *Zlatý fond denníka SME* (zlatyfond.sme.sk).

Hungarian rebel leader Imre Thököly, but also prominent Protestant townsmen suspected of disloyalty to the emperor in Vienna. After the siege of the city of Prešov in eastern Slovakia and its occupation by Habsburg forces in 1687, it was in particular this Protestant centre which suffered the consequences of Caraffa's special policy of revenge and persecution. In an atmosphere of intimidation, intrigue, and violence Caraffa made sure that eventually some twenty-four prominent Protestant citizens and local noblemen were executed in a gruesome way. In Slovak history these events became known as the 'Prešov slaughterhouse' (*prešovská jatka*), an episode in Counter-Reformation violence which, perhaps more than any other comparable episode from this period, served to illustrate the true nature of Catholic intolerance and Habsburg oppression.

Important in this connection was the fact that the bloodbath of 1687 led to the writing of an almost iconic Slovak manuscript that was published not long after the events, the *prešovská jatka* by the Slovak Lutheran teacher Ján Rezik.[33] This famous political tract from Upper Hungary made the name 'Karaffa', as Rezik spelled it, notorious for all times to come. It described in detail the most important events in and around Prešov, the intrigues used to produce 'evidence' against the accused, the character of Caraffa himself, and so on. There can be little doubt that, for Slavic and Magyar Protestants, the name 'Antonio Caraffa' and what was seen as the sinister background of Spanish-Italian cruelty became a key element in the shaping of a set of symbols and negative images, not only of the Catholic and Habsburg Counter-Reformation in general but in particular of its more extreme 'Hispanic' or 'Iberian' features lurking in the background. 'Sinister', 'cruel', 'arrogant' and the like are probably the right words, the most suitable symbolic terms to describe how the Lutherans and Calvinists of northern Hungary perceived the Iberian and Hispanic aspect of the war against them. And the *prešovská jatka* became the iconic text to help entrench this historical image.

---

[33] Rezik's text is available in *Zlatý fond* as well.

Conclusions

One conclusion that can be drawn from this brief investigation is that the contact or relationship between the Iberian world and the world of Slavic Central Europe was—apart from the Austrian Habsburgs—'mediated' to some degree by personalities from Spanish Italy, especially Naples. However, the Italian military commanders and instruments of Catholic repression in Protestant Slavic Europe were understood to be the representatives of the two pillars of international Habsburg Catholic power, Spain and Austria. While Protestant Czechs and Slovaks were most directly confronted with the Austrian Habsburg army, it seemed to many of them that the main political and ideological centre of the international Counter-Reformation was Iberia, i.e. Spain and its subordinate territories including those in Italy. Of course, it was the Austrian Habsburgs themselves who were the local, immediate enemy of the Protestant movements among the Czechs, Slovaks, and others, and who were responsible for the political decision to mobilise additional troops from the Spanish Empire or Spanish Italy. Yet, in symbolic terms it was the international power and influence of 'Imperial Spain'—even though its ruler in the seventeenth century was only a king—which often counted for more than did the power and status of the ruler of the Austrian Habsburg lands, the 'Holy Roman Emperor'. The emperor seemed to be rather impotent at times, being forced by his relative military and political weakness to call for help from his Spanish allies in Italy.

The consistent support of Spain (or 'Iberia' including Portugal) for Austria, i.e. the sustained cooperation between the two branches of the Habsburg dynasty, ensured that the forces of the Counter-Reformation in Central Europe were seen as hailing from Spain as much as from Vienna. The role played by a number of Spanish-Italian figures in Slavic and Hungarian Central Europe further contributed to the image of the tyrannical Hispanic power lurking behind Vienna. We have to keep in mind that, while the Habsburgs' 'a-Catholic' enemies in the Czech lands were practically annihilated after 1620, in Slovakia and some other regions in Hungary Protestantism survived to an extent that was of more than marginal significance. Slovak Lutheranism in the north and Magyar Calvinism in the north-east remained forces to be reckoned with for the Habsburg rulers and the Catholic Church. It was something that the Church and the Vienna Court could hardly change given that the ability to resist from these local Protestant bulwarks was considerable and deeply entrenched in political, social, and cultural positions. For various historical reasons, the project of Habsburg absolutism and total Catholic control could not be realised in Hungary after it had been implemented in Bohemia and Moravia. But this is another story and not part of the subject matter of this paper. What Czech and Slovak Protestants had in common, however, was the tendency to paint a picture of their religious and political enemy in which the 'Iberian' or 'Hispanic' factor played a prominent role. In this regard, they were acting quite similar to the Protestants of Western Europe. Spain, Portugal, and Iberia were the principal enemy of European Protestantism. This is something that must be taken into account when we want to deepen our understanding of mutual images and the 'relationship' between the Iberian and Slavic worlds.

4. Disaster and salvation: Jan Amos Komenský (1592-1670), António Vieira (1608-1697), and the meanings of seventeenth-century messianism

This essay analyses the phenomenon of missionary and messianic activity, thought, and writing by comparing two important figures from seventeenth-century Portugal and Slavic Central Europe. Jan Amos Komenský, the Moravian reformist theologian, philosopher, and pedagogue, believed that the suffering of the Czech people and his own Protestant group of the Unity of Brethren had a special role to play in unifying all true Christians and inaugurating a new era of general education, social justice, and human improvement. António Vieira, the great Jesuit messianic thinker and Brazilian missionary activist, believed that Portugal had to fulfil a special historical, political, and religious mission (i.e. the creation of the 'Fifth Empire') by which she would overcome her weakness and marginalisation, and the world would be saved from the miseries of folly, unbelief, and war.

Both men followed a difficult path in between the possibilities of human action and the presumed dependence on divine providence in a scheme of salvation history, part of which might be known through the revelations of contemporary prophets. Both were caught between the disasters that their respective nations had to suffer — Portugal at the hands of Spain and the Dutch; Bohemia-Moravia at the hands of the Austrian Habsburgs — and the ultimate salvation they believed was lying ahead thanks to God's grace as well as human effort. They managed to reconcile their religious and political activism with their understanding of human impotence by constructing a conception of messianic and millenarian faith, which served as an ideological and utopian extrapolation of their missionary activity. The rather unorthodox messianic ideas of both Komenský and Vieira brought them into conflict with more conservative actors and institutions in their own religious milieu. Both men were also important as first-class writers in various literary fields and produced a respectable body of religious, philosophical, political, pedagogic, and other works. This literature was an expression of their despair but also of their hopes, and was meant to promote their wide-ranging aims in an age of intellectual transition and confusion.[34]

Thus, our comparative analysis of the ideas of Komenský and Vieira is made against the background of missionary activity and messianic thought, both of which are to be understood in a broad sense. These phenomena have to be seen in the context of Christian expansionist universalism and an older Christian millenarian and messianic tradition, but also in the political context of the disasters that befell Portugal after its incorporation in the Spanish Empire in 1580 and Bohemia-Moravia after the victory of the Habsburg-led Counter-Reformation following the Battle of White Mountain in 1620. The two men with whom we are concerned were on opposite sides of the great religious divide in seventeenth-century Europe, and yet they had a lot in common. In contrast to Komenský and his religious minority group, Vieira operated on the side of the powerful Catholic Church, but within the Catholic world he represented a minority of radical Jesuits who protested against Portuguese

---

[34] For Komenský see Milada Blekastad, *Comenius. Versuch eines Umrisses von Leben, Werk und Schicksal des Jan Amos Komenský* (Oslo/Prague, 1969); Veit-Jakobus Dieterich, *Johann Amos Comenius* (Reinbek bei Hamburg, 1991); John Amos Comenius, 'The Bequest of the Unity of Brethren', in C.J. Wright, *Comenius and the Church Universal* (London, 1941), pp. 41-66; for Vieira see C.R. Boxer, *A Great Luso-Brazilian Figure: Padre António Vieira, S.J., 1608-1697* (London, 1957); José R. Maia Neto, 'Vieira's Epistemology of History', in Karl A. Kottman (ed.), *Millenarianism and Messianism in Early Modern European Culture, Vol. II. Catholic Millenarianism: From Savonarola to the Abbé Grégoire* (Dordrecht/Boston/London, 2001), pp. 79-89; Bernard McGinn, 'Forms of Catholic Millenarianism: A Brief Overview', in Kottman (ed.), *Millenarianism and Messianism in Early Modern European Culture, Vol. II*, pp. 1-13 passim; for the broader context see Karl A. Kottman, 'Introduction', in ibid., pp. xv-xvii; Richard H. Popkin, 'Introduction to the Millenarianism and Messianism Series', in John Christian Laursen and Richard H. Popkin (eds.), *Millenarianism and Messianism in Early Modern European Culture, Vol. IV. Continental Millenarians: Protestants, Catholics, Heretics* (Dordrecht/Boston/London, 2001), pp. vii-xiv; John Christian Laursen and Richard H. Popkin, 'Introduction', in Laursen and Popkin (eds.), *Millenarianism and Messianism in Early Modern European Culture, Vol. IV*, pp. xv-xx.

corruption and the exploitation of the Amerindian population in South America. Both Vieira and Komenský wanted to renew Christianity and to help improve man and society. Although Komenský (Comenius) is widely known as a Czech or Moravian pedagogue and school reformer, he was at least as important as a millenarian theologian, a 'pansophic' all-round philosopher, a philologist and versatile Czech and Latin author, and a staunchly anti-Habsburg and anti-Catholic political figure. Vieira is known — if internationally less so than Komenský — as an influential Jesuit in Portugal and Brazil, a diplomat and court advisor, and a political, social, and cultural critic. He advocated a more tolerant attitude to the Jews and the crypto-Jewish *conversos* or 'New Christians' than most Portuguese were willing to assume at the time, and he became famous as a defender of the freedom of indigenous Brazilians despite his attempts to impose the Catholic faith upon them. At the same time, Vieira was praised for his great abilities as an orator and a writer — Fernando Pessoa called him 'the emperor of the Portuguese language' — and indeed, both Komenský and Vieira were important literary figures in addition to their other qualities.

The two men had a strong 'missionary' and 'messianic' disposition because they believed that their religious institutions as well as their respective nations had a special mission to fulfil in Europe and the rest of the world. In accordance with an idiosyncratic version of the Christian historical worldview, Vieira believed that Portugal was destined to be the 'Fifth Empire' in world history — the successor to Assyria, Persia, Greece, and Rome (including the Holy Roman Empire) — in order to spread the Catholic faith around the globe and so help redeem humankind. Komenský saw his Unity of Brethren, as well as the Czech people as such, as a chosen group with a special mission to help bring about historical human improvement, Protestant unity, general education, and ultimately salvation, peace, and justice in the world. He had strong Christian-utopian, millenarian, and messianic tendencies and believed in the impending Second Coming of Christ and in, so to speak, an 'apocalyptic happy end' to the suffering of the Czechs and humankind. Vieira, as a good Catholic, had to be more cautious in expressing such potentially 'heretic' ideas and indeed was put under observation by his more conservative Catholic enemies because of his unorthodox messianic tendencies, which in the 1660s led to his condemnation by the Portuguese Inquisition and a period of imprisonment.[35]

Missionary movements and messianic thought: a closer look

The ideas of Komenský and Vieira can be clarified by looking more precisely at the nature of missionary movements and—as an extrapolation of this—messianic thought. By missionary movements we understand those religious or quasi-religious movements which pursue the objective of 'expansionist' mass conversion accompanied by cultural, social, and political change or radical transformation. This is to be achieved by changing the attitudes, consciousness, and way of life of large groups of people. Our two seventeenth-century cases are perhaps primarily concerned with the religious aspect, but it must be realised that both Komenský and Vieira were also strongly involved in questions of moral and cultural reform, and always tended to connect the religious with the social and political sphere.

More in general, and also with respect to the twentieth century with its many ideological and political mass movements, we often observe among missionary movements a combination of different objectives or a shift in emphasis over time from one critical objective to another. Expanding mass religious movements sometimes turn into social and political reform movements (e.g. some Protestant movements in Europe or Islamic movements in Asia), while political or nationalist movements may develop a quasi-religious fervour turning them into 'political religions' (e.g. certain forms of socialist or ethnic-minority movements). Religious or political missionary movements may centre around an influential or

---

[35] Dieterich, *Johann Amos Comenius*; Comenius, 'The Bequest of the Unity of Brethren'; Boxer, *A Great Luso-Brazilian Figure*; Maia Neto, 'Vieira's Epistemology of History'. McGinn, in 'Forms of Catholic Millenarianism', stresses that by 1600 millenarianism and unorthodox concepts of salvation history had become taboo in Catholic circles.

charismatic individual; around a powerful traditional institution or organised group of enthusiasts for a 'holy cause'; or around a new idea in terms of a universal, sectarian or 'elect' religion, nation, or other kind of collective subject. Religious, political-ideological, or nationalist movements can develop into messianic movements, i.e. movements which proclaim the imminent coming of a Messiah or Saviour, who will be instrumental in bringing about a radical transformation of the existing cultural-religious or socio-political situation and ensure an end to injustice, ignorance, and human suffering. When the Messiah has (or is said to have) already appeared and is recognised as such by a group of followers, it is strictly speaking not possible any longer to speak of a messianic movement, because the Saviour's actions are now those of a leader of a specific reformist or revolutionary missionary movement. The messianic movement may be bound to fail given man's shortcomings or impatience, but may also continue as an institutionalised religious or ideological tradition. In the case of political messianic movements the same holds true, but here the term 'messianic' is often equivalent to 'missionary' or 'highly idealistic', referring to a movement around a charismatic leader or inspiring doctrine. The point to bear in mind is that real—i.e. essentially religious—messianic movements live in anticipation of someone or something that has not yet come and likely never will, even if their supporters and believers think otherwise. It is hope, striving, and faith that matter, not real fulfilment. The archetype of all Messiahs, the Jewish one, is the most longstanding and consistent example of this. Indeed, all hopes and expectations notwithstanding, 'messianic man' realises he is impotent without divine help and intervention.[36] This is probably what separates messianic from quasi-messianic movements.

Thus, what is characteristic of essentially religious messianic movements and messianic thought—both Komenský and Vieira are examples of this—is that human actors are not believed to be

---

[36] Cf. Popkin, 'Introduction to the Millenarianism and Messianism Series'; Kottman, 'Introduction', in Kottman (ed.), *Millenarianism and Messianism in Early Modern European Culture, Vol. II*; Laursen and Popkin, 'Introduction', in Laursen and Popkin (eds.), *Millenarianism and Messianism in Early Modern European Culture, Vol. IV*.

capable of implementing any desired moral or political transformation on their own. They are dependent on divine intervention to assist them in this and to show them the way forward in one way or another. This may happen through the appearance of a new Messiah figure (but here the story becomes potentially heretical) or through the visions of some kind of prophet. This intermediary figure is not necessarily divine, half-divine, or even directly sent by God; however, he is usually seen as a critical part of 'God's plan', of 'divine providence'. He has his place and plays his role in the unfolding of salvation history; he may be one through whom the 'spirit of God' is speaking; and the divine voice or spirit may speak in fact through various prophetic figures. Indeed, the coming of a Saviour, Redeemer, or Messiah-like figure — and the demise of a mortal enemy — is often announced by such 'seers' or prophets, i.e. ordinary believers with a special gift to detect God's design or some aspect of it, either in a short-term or a longer-term perspective. While some predicted developments are of a more general historical kind, for example the special mission of an elect nation like the world-conquering Catholic Portuguese or the purifying post-Hussite Czechs, more specific prophetic predictions may involve the decisive intervention of a providential military leader or exceptional king. This might be the Swedish king Gustav Adolf who — according to Komenský — was going to defeat the Catholic armies in Germany in the Thirty Years' War and liberate Bohemia.[37] It might also be the Portuguese king João IV, who not only led the anti-Spanish Portuguese Restoration in 1640 but, according to Vieira, would rise from the dead long after his death in 1656 in order to proclaim the Portuguese Fifth Empire. However, such events figuring a 'secular Messiah' were only a prelude to the return of Christ himself, which meant the beginning of the End Time, the last Millennium, the final stage of human history. What we may call the 'messianic configuration' was a complex ideological construction comprising different

---

[37] At a later stage, in 1655, Komenský wrote a millenarian tract professing the belief that another Swedish king, Karl Gustav, would play the role of liberator of Bohemia; see Susanna Åkerman, 'Queen Christina of Sweden and Messianic Thought', in David S. Katz and Jonathan I. Israel (eds.), *Sceptics, Millenarians and Jews* (Leiden, 1990), pp. 142-60, here pp. 151-2.

kinds of individuals with their own unique role in the unfolding historical drama. It included a variety of ideas, all of which were a functional part of a comprehensive salvation history.

The messianic dynamics, religious and secular

The messianic configuration and its ideological dynamics included, first of all, leading thinkers who defined the general eschatological, historical, and political situation, in other words men like Vieira and Komenský. Secondly, there were individuals with prophetic qualities who were recognised by these religious and ideological leaders as true, authentic, divinely inspired prophets. Significant examples in the Portuguese case were the sixteenth- and seventeenth-century 'Sebastianists'. They included Manuel Bocarro-Rosales (probably a crypto-Jew) and, notably, the shoemaker Gonçalo Anes known as *O Bandarra*, whose only error according to Vieira was that he regarded the lost sixteenth-century King Sebastian instead of King João IV as Portugal's providential liberator and national Messiah.[38] Other examples are Christoph Kotter, Christina Poniatowska, and Mikuláš Drabík in the case of seventeenth-century Central Europe — people who were seen by Komenský as true prophets.[39] Drabík (like Komenský a Czech post-1620 exile) and others predicted the ultimate defeat of the Habsburgs and the Catholic Powers by elect Protestant leaders, some of whom were to play a historic role in this regard. Thirdly, indeed, there were political and military leaders with a special providential task to help create a more favourable situation for an oppressed nation or a particular religious group. A forth element were national and/or religious groups bearing the imprint of God's plan, for example the Portuguese Catholics and Jesuits or the Czech Brethren and Utraquists.

---

[38] See for the historical context surrounding King Sebastian David Birmingham, *A Concise History of Portugal* (Cambridge, 2003), pp. 36-7.
[39] Martin Mulsow, 'Who was the Author of the *Clavis apocalyptica* of 1651? Millenarianism and Prophecy between Silesian Mysticism and the Hartlib Circle', in Laursen and Popkin (eds.), *Millenarianism and Messianism in Early Modern European Culture, Vol. IV*, pp. 57-75 passim.

Fifth, there often was a messianic combination of apocalyptic, utopian, and millenarian expectations, which were to be fulfilled through a dramatic series of events with the ultimate end of bringing about moral regeneration, justice, peace, and salvation for the world or, more narrowly, the elect. Interestingly, while the elect were usually Christians, Jews might play a special role in the scheme of things as well. It was believed by some prophetic thinkers that the Jews would rebuild their temple in Jerusalem with Christian help and then convert to Christianity in a particular way, possibly by embracing the Christian faith while retaining certain Jewish traits. It is not difficult to imagine that the latter idea may have been of 'New Christian' provenance and that ex-Jewish prophets were playing their own role in the 'messianic game'.[40] Finally, there was a host of enemies to be fought, including the Muslim Turks, pseudo-Christian representatives of the Anti-Christ (according to Protestants, the Catholic Church), and various kinds of heretics (according to Catholics, the Protestant 'sects'). Missionary and messianic movements strongly encouraged a historical way of thinking, however flawed by religious doctrine. They were deeply concerned with change and historical time, even if these transformational dynamics were seen in terms of a divine plan or a scheme of salvation history that was essentially deterministic (either linear or cyclic) and not open-ended.

---

[40] Matt Goldish, 'Patterns in Converso Messianism', in Matt D. Goldish and Richard H. Popkin (eds.), *Millenarianism and Messianism in Early Modern European Culture, Vol. I. Jewish Messianism in the Early Modern World* (Dordrecht/Boston/London, 2001), pp. 41-63, and pp. 53-6 for Portuguese messianic thinkers like Fray Luis de León, a *converso* millenarian, Luis Días, who was arrested by the Inquisition for his 'Judaising' writings, and the probably crypto-Jewish *converso* Bocarro-Rosales. Vieira himself, who understood that the belief in non-canonical prophets was suspect, nevertheless, under the influence of *converso* thought, saw the *converso* and Jewish condition as a key to the Millennium. However, his final goal, of course, was the conversion of the Jews to Christianity. See Jonathan I. Israel, 'Dutch Sephardi Jewry, Millenarian Politics, and the Struggle for Brazil (1640-1654)', in Katz and Israel (eds.), *Sceptics, Millenarians and Jews*, pp. 76-97, here pp. 84-5. Among the Portuguese historians of *Sebastianismo* and seventeenth-century messianism (notably including the role of 'New Christians') are Elias Lipiner, J. Lúcio de Azevedo, Antonio José Saraiva, Francisco Moreno-Carvalho, and José R. Maia Neto.

As already noted, messianic and millenarian movements, even when primarily religious, could contain strong political and social tendencies or be deeply concerned with the liberation of a nation. Portugal had to be liberated from the Spanish yoke and from Dutch overseas aggression; Bohemia from the Catholic yoke and the Austrian Habsburgs.[41] Political or social groups involved in the articulation of messianic ideology might be the peasantry, poor townsmen, and of course some elite group that had been deprived of its former power and influence, such as the lower nobility or a section of the clergy. A charismatic leader was likely to come to the fore who understood the interests and perceptions of disaffected groups, but such a leader not always emerged spontaneously and sometimes had to be 'invented'. A nation or religious group might assume the attributes of a Messiah-like collective subject vis-à-vis the rest of society or even the world, claiming to be engaged in an historic task of redeeming humankind even if this implied imposing its (beneficial) supremacy upon it. Also in cases like this — Portugal making the world safe for Catholic Christianity; Czechs helping to purify and regenerate Christianity itself — messianic movements usually produced 'prophetic' individuals announcing the coming of a revolution or the inevitable because preordained success of a transformative undertaking. Thus, if in diverse ways, both religious and more secularly articulated messianic movements — and especially those that were a combination of both — tended to proclaim the coming of a Messiah-like leader or 'revolutionary actor'. This might be Christ himself in his Second Coming; a national, political, or religious leader ending the suffering of his people; or an elect group or religious vanguard who felt confident of their final victory even if only after a certain period of time.

The ideological leaders and prophetic seers of a messianic movement tried to convince the people around them and the broader masses of the truth of their 'apocalyptic' message, which

---

[41] See for Portuguese views on the seventeenth-century Dutch Protestant enemy Padre António Vieira, *Een natte hel: Brieven en preken van een Portugese jezuïet*, trans. and epilogue by Harrie Lemmens (Amsterdam/Antwerpen, 2001). This collection of letters and sermons by Vieira contains interesting information about another European cross-cultural topic.

represented a powerful source of hope. If this mobilisation proved successful, the movement and its leaders either remained within the limits of orthodox thought and behaviour or developed more unorthodox or 'heretical' tendencies (Vieira was accused of this). If messianic expectations were not fulfilled and people had to suffer disillusionment, messianic fervour might dissipate. But it was also possible that the belief in an imminent transformation of the religious or political world was so strong that the millenarian 'happy-end perspective' was sustained even if the reality seemed to contradict it.

Komenský, Vieira, and the seventeenth century

The seventeenth century is an important period in European history as far as the inspiring power of missionary and messianic movements and their charismatic leaders is concerned. What also made the century significant is that it was an age of transition from a world dominated by religion to a more 'secular' and 'scientific' one. However, it would be a mistake to think that religion and science were necessarily opposites in the seventeenth century; that religious traditions were in the process of disappearing; or that the new 'empirical', 'rational', 'scientific', 'secular' or 'sceptical' outlook was about to triumph on all fronts of intellectual and cultural life. On the contrary, it is clear that the different forms of Christian religion not only survived but were renewed and adapted to the new insights and preoccupations. The ways in which this happened and the growing influence of new philosophical and scientific ideas (experimental empiricism, mechanistic rationalism, new forms of political and social critique) meant that a new balance of religious and secular thought had to be developed by Europeans, including Central European Slavs and Iberians. The political or religious disasters suffered by nations like the Portuguese and the Czechs made these new challenges even more pressing and complex at the time, and complicate their historical analysis today. A situation of national crisis—Portugal's subordination to Spain, or Protestant Bohemia's subjection to Catholic Austria—could strengthen national traditions but also force intellectual and religious leaders to rethink some of their old concepts.

The reformist and Protestant personality of Komenský is an important example of the new seventeenth-century trends in pedagogic and social philosophy, while Vieira was a leading exponent of a more critical trend in the Catholic world. Vieira not only rejected the exploitation and oppression of indigenous Brazilians, but also the Catholic fundamentalist intolerance of the Jews and Jewish *conversos* as well as the unsavoury influence and practices of the Inquisition. He advocated a more broad-minded and irenic Catholicism, even though he was a militant Catholic missionary who believed that Portugal and the Jesuits had a special mission to fulfil in converting the world, which even might include using the sword. Komenský's ideas were different from those of Vieira mainly in the sense that he believed that the evil of the Catholic Church had to be replaced by a truly reformed Christian religion. Like Vieira, he believed that war was sometimes inevitable to achieve the aim of overcoming the most dangerous spiritual and political enemy. As far as the attitude of the Jesuits to modern science is concerned, it is hardly necessary to remind ourselves that they actually played a major part in developing some of the new scientific disciplines and reconciling them with Christian faith. They were truly a cultural and intellectual vanguard as well as a social and political one, and their hatred of the Inquisition was well known. Komenský, a leader of the Czech Brethren whose aim was to reintegrate science and religion, believed that the Brethren — similar to the Jesuits in the view of educated Catholics — were a kind of harbingers of the better, more pious, more just, and more intelligent world of the future. The Czech people, the Brethren, he himself, and Protestant leaders like the King of Sweden or even some Hungarian aristocratic anti-Habsburg rebels were destined to play their part in the coming transformation of the world. Despite all the wars and religious conflicts in Europe, this transformation would have a Christian-humanist character and both Komenský and Vieira, for all their differences, were concerned to promote Christian ideals as well as social and political reforms.

Because both men believed they had a special mission to fulfil within the framework of salvation history, both displayed a tendency to move from a 'missionary' to a 'messianic' perspective on what they saw as the necessary transformation of the world, the divinely determined course of human history, and indeed the events of the near future. For both Vieira and Komenský having a sense of mission was not enough: they believed in a messianic way that their strivings and activities were part of a larger, preordained scheme of divine providence whose ultimate end was redemption and salvation, peace and justice, not only in heaven but on earth. They believed in human 'activism' but also in the partly known, partly unknown workings of a divine salvation history which included incomprehensible adverse events. However, some of these imminent events — especially those of a more positive nature — could be predicted and explained by visionary prophets. Vieira himself wrote a series of visionary messianic works including *História do Futuro, Esperanças de Portugal, Quinto Império do Mundo, Primeira e segunda vida de El-rei Dom João o quarto,* and *Clavis Prophetarum*. These sought to connect biblical and contemporary prophecies regarding the immediate future and to balance disastrous events and divine punishment of human sin with positive hope and the certainty of ultimate redemption and glory. Komenský did much the same thing. In 1650 he wrote in his Testament of the Unity of Brethren: 'I trust God that after the passing of the storm of wrath which our sins brought down upon our heads, the rule of thine affairs shall again be restored to thee, O Czech people.'[42] The road to salvation was not an easy one, yet it was there.

Concluding observations

Insofar as man was not in control of his own affairs — and this was believed to be the case to an overwhelming degree — the world could be depicted as a theatre directed by God, who alone has the power to ensure a happy end to an unhappy stage-play. Komenský produced a remarkable example of this philosophical view in his

---

[42] Comenius, 'The Bequest of the Unity of Brethren', p. 61.

Consultatio catholica, the 'General Consultation on the Improvement of Human Affairs', a work in which he sought to synthesise his encyclopaedic Pansophic thought comprising theology, philosophy, science, and pedagogy. His 'Pansophia' as a whole was gradually developed to embrace the most diverse dimensions of human existence and human knowledge, of human misery and stubborn optimism. *The Labyrinth of the World and the Paradise of the Heart* included observations on the folly of the world and the consolation of inner life. Komenský and Vieira were equally depressed by the human folly around them despite their religious optimism, and Vieira dared to observe that the curing of folly was unfortunately not among the miracles performed by Christ. Komenský, who defended the prophecies of Kotter, Poniatowska, Drabík, and others in works like *De veris ac falsis prophetis*, 'History of Revelations', and *Lux in tenebris*, found the strength to proclaim in his *Via lucis* that in spite of all disasters there was 'no greater consolation than the old promises of God about the light at the end of time'.[43]

Thus, even though the two men came from very different backgrounds, there were some remarkable similarities between them, regarding their ways of thinking, feeling, and acting. Of course, this could be explained by the longer Christian tradition they shared, which was significant despite all the reformist and intellectual changes of the seventeenth century and all the cultural, doctrinal, and social differences between the religious milieus of Vieira and Komenský and between Portugal and Central Europe. This tells us a lot about the condition of seventeenth-century 'Christian Europe' as observed by the more sensitive and educated type of passionate believer. The messianic tendencies of Komenský and Vieira were sometimes extreme, but often enough they were counterbalanced by critical considerations. Such was the age and such were the possibilities for co-existence of religion and rational thought. The biblical prophets — Isaiah, Elijah (Elias), or Nathan — had the same significance for Catholics and Protestants, which could encourage a degree of respect for Jewish traditions even

---

[43] See for this and other 'optimistic' messianic statements Dieterich, *Johann Amos Comenius*; Mulsow, 'Who was the Author of the *Clavis apocalyptica* of 1651?'

among some Catholics. At the same time, the contemporary 'prophets' invoked by Komenský and Vieira were total opposites, as were their confessional and political ideals.

The differences and similarities between Komenský and Vieira were expressed in their writings, which embraced the different literary genres of the age and their respective religious and intellectual milieus. Both Komenský and Vieira were conscious of the limits to what human beings can accomplish and of their dependence on God and His plan with man and the world. In conclusion, it seems fitting to quote an impressive passage from Komenský's *Consultatio catholica*, which was supposedly written in the 1660s and with which Vieira might have agreed if he had enjoyed the opportunity to respond to it. It refers to man's existential impotence and his dependence on God, and to the fact that he is like an observer of his own life, like a spectator in a theatre. While the missionary and messianic mind is strongly motivated to engage in purposeful action, it is also keenly aware of how little man can achieve on his own. But this is no reason for despair or pessimism, perhaps rather the opposite. Komenský speaks of God as 'the poet of drama', 'the heavenly artist'. This poet and artist of the universe will ensure a happy end to the dramatic story of humankind:

> At first sight the organisation and guidance of the world do much resemble a stage-play, one that the wisdom of God is playing with the sons of men ... And nothing is more typical of a play than that the spectators, who at the start do hardly understand what it aims at, by surprising developments and after all of them have come to anticipate a catastrophe, are finally made to understand what was enacted and what is the redeeming outcome that was prepared, which is now becoming ever more clear to all. Thus the poet of drama finally receives applause for his artistic ability, as the happy end which he has found to resolve all the confusion has become visible to the eyes of all. In earnest, is it appropriate to expect less of the heavenly artist? ... What, then, could reasonably not be expected of his acts which conclude the great drama he plays with the human race?[44]

---

[44] *Consultatio catholica*, quoted in Dieterich, *Johann Amos Comenius*, p. 117 (our translation into English).

5. The miracle of Maurício: multicultural toleration and decolonising tendencies in seventeenth-century Brazil

> The quiet and preservation of the colony of Brazil depends in part on the friendship of the Indians. With this in mind they should be permitted to enjoy their natural freedom ... Orders should be issued that they are not outraged by their commandeurs, hired out for money or forced to work in sugar mills against their will. Each [Indian] should, on the contrary, be allowed to live in the way he understands, and to work where he wishes like men of our nation.
>
> (Johan Maurits of Nassau, September 1644)[45]

> So come to our side while there is still time, so that with the help of our friends we can live together in this land which is our home and in the bosom of all our family. We are all agreed about this. Therefore come and join us, and I assure you that the Dutch will give you the same benefits as they do us. Have not the slightest doubt; the Portuguese will slip away; those bandits will disappear like the wind.
>
> (Pieter Poti, Potiguar leader, October 1645)[46]

If 'decolonising hegemonic thought' — a concept used by some cultural critics — is considered a task of post-colonial cultural criticism, then the critical analysis of historiography and indeed of colonial history itself should be part of this endeavour as well. In this context, the history of seventeenth-century Brazil is greatly illuminating, because its complexity and political and cultural contradictions provide important evidence for the thesis that there actually was no simple hegemonic structure in colonial society or in colonial

---

[45] Johan Maurits of Nassau, Report to the States General of the United Netherlands, 27 September 1644, quoted in John Hemming, *Red Gold: The Conquest of the Brazilian Indians* (2nd ed., London, 1995), pp. 296, 614. Hemming's reference is to José António Gonçalves de Mello, *Tempo dos flamengos: influência da ocupação holandesa na vida e na cultura do norte do Brasil* (Rio de Janeiro, 1947), pp. 234-5, still one of the most important works in the Portuguese language on the 'Dutch period' in Brazil.

[46] Pieter Poti to António Felipe Camarão, another indigenous leader, 31 October 1645, quoted in Hemming, *Red Gold*, pp. 310, 618, where reference is made to Pedro Souto Maior, 'Fastos Pernambucanos', *Revista do Instituto Histórico e Geographico Brasileiro* 76 (Rio de Janeiro, 1913), pp. 153-6, an important early Portuguese-language publication based on Dutch sources.

discourse and ideology. Nor was there a lack of will or capacity on the part of colonised 'non-Europeans' or other non-dominant groups to contest such systems of European power and domination as officially existed.

The historiography of colonial Brazil of the past half century has given ample attention to the complexities that need to be addressed and cannot be said to be lacking in depth, quality, or will to be 'objective' and multidimensional, having evidently overcome the worst colonial and ethnocentric distortions of the past. That groups like indigenous Brazilians,[47] black slaves, or immigrant Jews were not just victims but active participants in the historical drama and capable of defining their own interests, is generally recognised today. It is also understood that among the dominant groups in mid-seventeenth-century Brazil, notably the Portuguese and Dutch administrations as well as European settlers and various cultural and religious agents, there was no unanimous perspective on colonial policy. Some Portuguese Jesuits actively opposed settler attitudes towards the indigenous peoples, while enlightened Dutch administrators criticised those of short-sighted merchants and puritan Calvinists. Among the dilemmas faced by colonial administrators, religious institutions, and other groups of Europeans was the question of whether certain indigenous Brazilians, or for that matter free blacks or immigrant Jews, should have the right to enjoy a degree of independence, freedom, and 'otherness'. This contradicted the more control-oriented idea that all must know their place in a colonial society with a distinct hierarchical structure and a more or less homogeneous religious and cultural identity. This dilemma was never resolved by any actor in the Brazilian labyrinth, influenced as it was by opportunistic considerations and conflicting interests as well as different ways of life, religious traditions, and cultural perspectives.

During the period of 1630-54 the political and ethno-cultural complexity of Brazilian society further increased as the Dutch West-

---

[47] Although the term 'Amerindians' is sometimes used to refer to the native peoples of the American continent, we will generally speak of indigenous Brazilians considering that each expression has its pros and cons and that even an author like John Hemming uses the latter term.

India Company (WIC) occupied a part of north-east Brazil centred on Recife, introducing policies and patterns of social and cultural behaviour that posed a threat to Portuguese hegemony in Brazil. Especially during the rule of Governor Johan Maurits van Nassau-Siegen ('Maurício') in 1637-44, the Dutch administration succeeded in gaining the friendship and support of various indigenous peoples and even a part of the black and mixed-race population. They also pursued a policy of religious toleration which enabled the Jews (settled Portuguese crypto-Jews as well as newly arrived Dutch Jews) and the settled Catholic population to live in peace alongside the newly dominant Protestants. All of this had consequences for prevailing notions of power structure, group identity, and inter-group relations. The multicultural segmentation and social complexity of colonial society increased as a result of the new more enlightened and pragmatic policies, which were partly motivated by expediency and strategic considerations but, to some extent, also by new principles of toleration of diversity and freedom of conscience, which were characteristic of the more 'liberal' type of Calvinist of which Johan Maurits was an example. The struggle for Brazil between the Portuguese and the Dutch created a new constellation of political forces and opportunities, which provided several non-dominant groups in the colony with new possibilities for resistance in their struggle for freedom. This held true for a broad range of ethnic, religious, and social groups including independent or semi-independent indigenous peoples, imported Africans in various social positions, and local 'New Christians' who could join the community of Jewish immigrants from Amsterdam (themselves often of Portuguese origin). The category of Africans included black soldiers, slaves, and free mixed-race individuals, some of whom took the Portuguese and others the Dutch side, with each of the groups involved expecting certain advantages from the choice they made.

Maurício's period of administration came to an end in 1644, and so did the Dutch period in Brazilian history (1654), but the legacy of this historical episode may have had a long-term impact on the consciousness of Brazilians in the north-east. Part of this, perhaps, was a greater sensitivity to social and multicultural toleration, or even a 'decolonising tendency' in the sense of a more conscious rejection of existing hegemonic structures and extreme inequalities. This did not prevent the system of colonial slavery and racial inequality from being consolidated almost everywhere, including, not much later, in Dutch Surinam. The Dutch, of course, were no better than the Portuguese, but their different historical experience and greater pragmatism promoted, in some situations, less rigid policies, and the figure of Maurício did the rest. While the memory of Maurício may have played a part in encouraging some people in Portuguese Brazil to envisage a more tolerant society, the peculiar moment of 'decolonisation' (or 're-colonisation') of 1654 may have set a precedent, especially through 'Pernambuco nationalism', sustained indigenous resistance, and slave revolts, for later moments of temporary or 'relative decolonisation' in Brazilian history. These included the runaway-slave republic of Palmares between the 1670s and 1690s; formal independence in 1822 and the historic moment of 1889 with its new republican and egalitarian (though not non-racial) ethos; and different moments in the twentieth century when mixed-race and black Brazilians began to contest the racial hierarchy. Perhaps it is possible to say that the 'Maurício episode' had demonstrated what could be done in terms of 'de-hegemonising' aspects of inequality in Brazilian society. Even if Dutch Brazil itself was hardly more than a case of 're-colonisation', some of Maurício's policies helped to temporarily remove features of the old Portuguese political, cultural, and racial hegemony. The resulting void was partly filled by the response of non-European and non-Catholic groups who used the opportunity to demand a degree of social equality and more tolerable forms of coexistence. This new promise, it may be argued, was one of the legacies of 'Maurício o Brasileiro'.[48]

---

[48] A classical Dutch biography of Johan Maurits added the nickname 'Brazilian' to his name following an older tradition; see P.J. Bouman, *Johan Maurits van Nassau, de Braziliaan* (Utrecht, 1947). In another publication the open-minded and culturally tolerant but also ambitious and glory-seeking Johan Maurits has been described as a 'humanist prince'; see E. van den Boogaart (ed.) in collaboration with H.R. Hoetink and P.J.P. Whitehead, *Johan Maurits van Nassau-Siegen 1604-1679: A Humanist Prince in Europe and Brazil* (The Hague, 1979). In the introduction to this notable collection of essays Hoetink speaks of the 'modernity' of Johan Maurits, i.e. his forward-looking, 'secular', and 'rational' orientation.

Seventeenth-century Brazil

This essay outlines how this 'promise' may have originated during the second quarter of the seventeenth century. Its aim is not primarily an account of the 'Dutch Brazil episode'—even though it includes such historical description as is necessary—but to revisit some of the crucial questions regarding the legacy of colonialism, historiographic debate, and the claims of 'decolonising thought'. We are concerned with the nature of the new dynamics engendered by the emergence of 'Dutch Brazil' alongside 'Portuguese Brazil'; the question of what this meant in terms of new opportunities for non-European and colonial subaltern groups to act as historical agents, especially for certain groups of indigenous Brazilians; and the dilemmas and contradictions that both the Dutch and the Portuguese were confronted with as a consequence of the Dutch invasion and the wars between the two colonial powers. These dilemmas concerned in part the sphere of cultural and religious policy and included the nature of strategic alliances with indigenous peoples or other non-European groups. They also involved disagreements within the two European dominant groups with regard to colonial ideology and politics.

It is not claimed that all these questions can be satisfactorily resolved in this essay, which is not meant as an original contribution to historiography but rather as a contribution to our reflections on colonial and post-colonial historical interpretation. The paper argues that colonial history itself, the older but especially the more recent historiography, and our own evaluations from the present 'post-colonial' perspective are all closely intertwined. We cannot say that 'history speaks for itself', nor can we reasonably claim we always know better than those who were involved themselves. As for the historiography of colonial and Dutch Brazil, we have to admit that its quality and interpretative orientation have greatly improved in recent decades. This literature is indispensable for all those who wish to understand colonial history or say anything sensible about its meaning and legacy, including the evolution of post-colonial and multicultural Brazil. It should help us to avoid cultivating simplistic and ahistorical claims and interpretations. What is especially important is to understand the dynamics of anti-colonial resistance and the limits of European colonial power.

Visions of social and political change and anti-colonial resistance in seventeenth-century Brazil existed among different population groups and included different perspectives. In Portuguese Brazil before 1630, various indigenous groups—especially those called 'Tapuia'[49]—continued to fight against the Portuguese and Brazilian colonial masters both on the frontier and deeper in the interior, and all European rivals or enemies of the Portuguese—the French, English, and Dutch—were keen to win their support. Other groups had settled in the Jesuit-controlled villages known as *aldeias*. Most of these indigenous peoples of coastal north-east Brazil belonged to the language group called 'Tupi', whose members had become more submissive and were partly acculturated to Jesuit Portuguese patterns. But because their incorporation into colonial society was by no means complete, neither in cultural nor economic terms, they continued to display forms of resistance such as refusing to work on unacceptable European terms or fully embrace the Christian religion and colonial ideology of stratification. Furthermore, black slaves working on the Pernambuco sugar estates and in other areas of north-east Brazil often tried to escape. In the second half of the seventeenth century the Palmares community of runaway slaves and other 'marginal' colonial elements became a notorious phenomenon. Part of the *mulatto* and *mameluco* mixed-race population of free black people, former slaves, and other people of colour by no means expressed contentment with their position either. The 'New Christians' also known as *conversos* or *marranos* (often crypto-Jews) were another story that was specific to the Catholic Portuguese and Spanish world including Iberian colonial society. They were—though in Brazil, perhaps, to a less extent—not only victims of religious persecution but also of the idea of Christian 'purity of blood'—an ideological invention which had come to prevail in the Portuguese world almost as much as in the Spanish.

---

[49] We follow the spelling of names like 'Tapuia' or 'Tupi' as adopted by authors like Fausto and Hemming. See Boris Fausto, *A Concise History of Brazil*, trans. by Arthur Brakel (Cambridge, 1999); Hemming, *Red Gold*.

While Catholic Portuguese Brazil may have been a relatively easygoing society as far as the general phenomenon of miscegenation was concerned, this was certainly not the case with respect to the almost caste-like social distinctions, racial prejudice (especially against people of African descent), and the ideology of European hegemony and superiority.[50] The Dutch intruders were not much better than the Portuguese and, at a later stage, possibly even worse. But during the Dutch Brazil episode they appeared to be in some respects more flexible and tolerant than the Portuguese. Perhaps these were pragmatic characteristics of a nation which had only recently begun to embark on colonial adventures.

If the Dutch wanted to have a chance to replace the Portuguese as the hegemonic power in Brazil, they would have to conduct a policy of greater social, religious, and 'multicultural' toleration towards at least *some* groups in Brazilian society or on the Brazilian frontier. This might strengthen their position in short-term strategic and military terms, or even consolidate their political, economic, and cultural-religious position in the long run. The idea in the new Dutch Republic was to use Brazil as a strategic base from which the Spanish Empire, which until 1640 included the Portuguese territories as well, could be more effectively attacked. Brazil would also be a source of wealth (especially because of the sugar plantations) and, possibly, a territory where Dutch and German colonists could be settled. To achieve this aim, the Dutch West India Company established in 1621, decided that the future colonial administration, and private settlers ('freeburghers') would have to ensure a measure of toleration of other population groups in Brazil. This concerned the freedom, autonomy, and cultural identity of different indigenous groups, but also of the socially dominant Portuguese and colonial Catholics and groups like the Jewish immigrants and local 'New Christians'. (Indeed, the Jewish community in Recife, the centre of Dutch Brazil, and other places quickly began to grow in the 1630s as numbers of Portuguese Jews from Amsterdam began to

---

[50] See e.g. C. R. Boxer, *Race Relations in the Portuguese Colonial Empire 1415-1825* (Oxford, 1963), pp. 86-130; Lyle N. McAlister, *Spain and Portugal in the New World, 1492-1700* (Minneapolis, 1984), esp. pp. 411-9; Fausto, *A Concise History of Brazil*, pp. 25-30.

arrive and many 'New Christians' openly reverted to the Jewish religion.) Even the more intricate question of the status of the black and slave population had to be paid close attention to; and indeed, an improvement of their lot was considered initially.

Thus, the weakness but also the strength of the Dutch was that they were newcomers to Brazil and, therefore, dependent to some extent on the support of less privileged sections of the colonial population and frontier indigenous peoples. An exception to this was the longstanding Dutch involvement in the sugar trade, which had been conducted in the past through *marrano* middlemen from Porto and Viana with whom the Dutch traditionally entertained good relations. A further source of Dutch strength was that the Dutch administration in Brazil and a part of the non-Jewish newcomers were strongly inclined to tolerate the Jews, including the old-established ones. With their knowledge of the Portuguese language and colonial society, the latter were an important element in the complex Brazilian political and multicultural landscape.

As already noted, the Dutch were also ready on strategic grounds to assume a relatively tolerant attitude towards the indigenous Brazilians. Some of their leaders had even been taken to the Netherlands after the unsuccessful Dutch attack on and subsequent withdrawal from Bahia in 1625 with the aim of receiving political and religious instruction in anticipation of the invasion of Pernambuco, further to the north, in 1630. The most famous of them was Pieter Poti (Pedro Potí), a Potiguar Tupi chief from Paraíba who led a contingent of indigenous warriors fighting on the side of the Dutch and kept sending letters to persuade other indigenous chiefs to join them. This did not mean that the Dutch always respected indigenous Brazilians and their culture more than they respected the Catholic Portuguese or Brazilian blacks; some of the colonisers allegedly held indigenous Brazilians in lower regard than the West Africans.[51] But others developed a strong sympathy for them in the 1630s and 1640s, including Johan Maurits van Nassau himself and

---

[51] Ernst van den Boogaart, 'Colour Prejudice and the Yardstick of Civility: the Initial Dutch Confrontation with Black Africans, 1590-1635', in Robert Ross (ed.), *Racism and Colonialism: Essays on Ideology and Social Sructure* (Leiden, 1982), pp. 33-54, here esp. 47, 54.

a number of 'commandeurs' — Dutch government agents, some of whom were married to indigenous women.[52] While a considerable proportion of black and mixed-race Brazilians, indigenous Tupi, and even some Tapuia remained loyal to the Portuguese, many others were anxious to support the new invaders. On either side, this was a strategic decision for those who were not simply forced to serve as soldiers or carriers. They were hoping to be rewarded with an improvement of their status or to be granted their freedom. The fate of Brazil would depend on the attitude of these non-Europeans to the military and political developments in the colony.

'Divine justice will intervene'

It is remarkable that on the eve of the 1630 invasion of the Brazilian captaincy of Pernambuco, the Dutch seem to have been confident that they would be supported, not only by the crypto-Jewish *marranos* in Olinda and Recife but also by anti-Portuguese indigenous Brazilians and even by the black slaves, who were expected to rise against their Portuguese masters.[53] At this stage, the Dutch themselves had not yet become major slave traders or slaveholders, but this was to change soon after they got hold of the larger Pernambuco sugar plantations in the mid-1630s. Indeed, they understood they would have to conciliate the Portuguese estate owners in order to keep sugar production going, which contradicted the idea of improving the status of the black slaves, especially since the indigenous Brazilians were to be protected against any attempt to enslave them. When the conquest of north-east Brazil began, the position of the Dutch was initially confined to the coastal areas of Pernambuco and the captaincies further to the north, with the Portuguese putting up stiff resistance.

---

[52] Hemming, *Red Gold*, pp. 293-6; Frans Leonard Schalkwijk, *The Reformed Church in Dutch Brazil (1630-1654)* (Zoetermeer, 1998), pp. 41, 49, 53, 210-1.
[53] Charles R. Boxer, *De Nederlanders in Brazilië 1624-1654*, trans. by H.G. Nijk (Alphen aan den Rijn, 1977), p. 27. This Dutch translation of Boxer's *The Dutch in Brazil 1624-1654* (1957) contains the original text where Dutch sources are quoted.

However, a degree of demoralisation may already have existed among part of the older colonial population. When the Franciscan friar Manoel Calado criticised the corruption and degeneration of Brazilian colonial society in his book *O valeroso Lucideno e triunfo da liberdade* (1648), he referred to the prophetic warning of a Dominican friar who had declared shortly before the invasion of the Dutch that they would come as a punishment for this corruption: 'for when there is no justice on earth, divine justice will intervene.'[54] This could be seen as an ex post facto explanation for the Brazilian crisis, but it is clear that among leading Catholic figures, especially the Portuguese Jesuits, Franciscans, and Dominicans, there was a strong awareness of the wrongs of Brazilian society. In the case of some of them—notably the Jesuit António Vieira—this also included criticism of Portuguese policy with regard to the Jews. After the 1630 invasion wealthy *marrano* merchants in Portugal were forced to provide loans for an armada against the Dutch. When in 1649 a similar policy was introduced once again through the establishment of the *Companhia do Brasil*, António Vieira, disliked by many Portuguese as 'a friend of the Jews', persuaded the Portuguese king to give the *marranos* guarantees that their property would not be confiscated by the Inquisition.[55]

In addition to Jews and indigenous Brazilians, by 1631 the WIC troops in Brazil also included black soldiers. In April 1632 the desertion to the Dutch of Domingos Fernandes Calabar, an influential figure of mixed-race heritage, proved to be crucial in turning the military tide to the favour of the invaders, with several hundred black fighters, mostly runaway slaves, joining them. Even more important was the fact that the Dutch were actively working for an alliance with several Tapuia groups in the interior of the captaincies

---

[54] Ibid., p. 53.
[55] George D. Winius, 'Two Lusitanian Variations on a Dutch Theme: Portuguese Companies in Times of Crisis, 1628-1662', in Leonard Blussé and Femme Gaastra (eds.), *Companies and Trade: Essays on Overseas Trading Companies during the Ancien Régime* (Leiden, 1981), pp. 119-34, esp. 125-9; Evaldo Cabral de Mello, *De Braziliaanse affaire. Portugal, de Republiek der Verenigde Nederlanden en Noord-Oost Brazilië, 1641-1669*, trans. by Catherine Barel (Zutphen, 2005), Chapters 3-4 passim. Vieira was seen by Portuguese public opinion as a friend of the Jews for various reasons.

of Pernambuco, Paraíba, Rio Grande do Norte, and Ceará. Especially their friendship with Tarairiu, the leader of a cannibal tribe much feared by the Portuguese, was a remarkable feat. Other Tapuia remained loyal to the Portuguese, in particular to the Portuguese administrator Martím Soares Moreno, who had a special relationship with some of them. However, it would seem that most Tapuia groups who participated in the war between the Portuguese and the Dutch took the side of the latter. The more acculturated Tupi were divided as well, even if in their case a majority remained on the Portuguese side, especially those who were led by the notorious indigenous leader António Felipe Camarão. But in Paraíba and Rio Grande do Norte, the Tupi from the local *aldeias* went over to the Dutch in January 1635, providing several hundred additional soldiers after the desertion of their Jesuit patron Manuel de Morais. (Morais later went to Holland, married there, and then came back to Brazil; he finally ended up before the Inquisition.[56]) At the same time, part of the Portuguese *moradores* (rural colonists and estate owners) gradually warmed towards the Dutch rule, encouraged by promises of religious freedom and respect for their property. Also, Catholic friars began to collaborate with the Dutch authorities, the Franciscan Calado and the Jesuit Morais being examples of this in different ways. Some did so for tactical and pragmatic reasons, others on grounds perhaps more difficult to understand, which may have included resentment of aspects of their life under the old regime.

The Brazilian historian and political scientist Boris Fausto has described the extent of indigenous support for the Dutch invaders in terms that seem to overestimate rather than underestimate it:

---

[56] E. van den Boogaart, 'De Nederlandse expansie in het Atlantische gebied 1590-1674', in E. van den Boogaart and M.A.P. Meilink-Roelofsz (eds.), *Overzee. Nederlandse koloniale geschiedenis 1590-1975* (Haarlem, 1982), pp. 113-144, here 119-20, 125-6; Hermann Wätjen, *Das holländische Kolonialreich in Brasilien. Ein Kapitel aus der Kolonialgeschichte des 17. Jahrhunderts* (The Hague/Gotha, 1921), pp. 61-2, 254-7; Boxer, *De Nederlanders in Brazilië*, pp. 68, 75; Hemming, *Red Gold*, pp. 299-302; Schalkwijk, *The Reformed Church in Dutch Brazil*, p. 41. According to Schalkwijk, the mixed-race leader Calabar became a member of the Reformed Church; Morais may have made the same step.

> Because of his importance, Calabar has been recognised as the great traitor of the first phase of the war. But he was not alone. In fact, the Dutch could always count on local support—from different plantation owners and cane growers, as well as from people poorly integrated into Portuguese colonial society or from those totally outside it. New Christians, black slaves, Tapuia Indians, and poor, destitute mixed-bloods aided the Dutch. It is true that Camarão's Indians and Henrique Dias's blacks sided with the Luso-Brazilians. However, these mobilizations were relatively small.[57]

Other historians have made observations on the collaborationist phenomenon as well. J.H. Parry, for example, writes that the Dutch 'made valuable allies among the Amerindians, some of whom thus found means of expressing a longstanding hostility to the Portuguese'.[58] Crucial in another way was the Catholic clergy, which the Protestant Dutch tried to neutralise when it became clear that they could not win them over. From about 1635, the secular clergy and some of the Franciscans, Benedictines, and others were openly tolerated in the Dutch-controlled territory. Some of them appeared more supportive of the Dutch authorities than would initially have been expected, notably Father Calado, who assisted in the rapprochement between the Dutch and the Portuguese *moradores*. The Franciscan Calado later wrote in his *Valeroso Lucideno* that the Dutch admiral Jan Cornelisz Lichthart—who apparently wanted to do his bit in the rapprochement—had told the Portuguese he was a 'crypto-Catholic', possibly to help them overcome their mistrust. However, the offer of toleration was not extended to the Jesuits, who had been instructed by their Provincial (district overseer) to leave the Dutch-occupied territory and who were seen by the Dutch as an evil force that had encouraged the indigenous inhabitants of the *aldeias* to fight against them. An exception was the eccentric case of the Jesuit Morais, who, after he surrendered with his *aldeia*, began to show an interest in the Calvinist religion and to support the Dutch Reformed Church. He also gave a lot of useful information about Brazilian conditions. But while some Dutchmen and colonial Portuguese found a way to co-exist, Pernambuco's

---

[57] Fausto, *A Concise History of Brazil*, p. 44.
[58] J.H. Parry, *The Age of Reconnaissance: Discovery, Exploration and Settlement 1450-1650* (London, 1973), p. 323.

governor Mathias de Albuquerque withdrew to Bahia with more than 7,000 soldiers and civilians following the Dutch occupation. Perhaps the most dramatic episode of this withdrawal in 1635 was the capture by Luso-Brazilian forces of the 'traitor' Calabar, who seems to have been executed in a gruesome way.[59]

In January 1637 Johan Maurits of Nassau arrived in Recife, and soon there were at least a thousand indigenous Brazilians fighting on the Dutch side. Apart from the work of his predecessors, this may have been a natural result of his talent for negotiating with indigenous leaders and keeping their loyalty. The religious freedom given to the Jews seemed to him a matter of course, and the freedom allowed to Catholics even included the holding of processions, something that was not permitted in the Dutch Republic. The Portuguese in Dutch Brazil were brought within the scope of Roman-Dutch Law, being accorded the same civic rights, having to pay the same taxes etc. This did not mean that all Dutchmen were happy with this situation, neither with the freedom for Catholics nor indeed for the Jews. But Johan Maurits ignored most objections of the more intolerant among the Calvinist pastors and other critics of his liberal policies. An interesting measure taken was the admittance to Dutch Brazil of a group of French Capuchin friars, who soon expressed their contempt for the ignorance of the local Catholic clergy. But they also observed that the Catholic zeal of the Portuguese was by no means weakened by this ignorance; it was obviously a question of cultural patriotism rather than pure religion.

Most difficult to resolve in Dutch Brazil was the status of the black slaves. It was decided that those who had run away from the Portuguese to the Dutch before the Portuguese surrendered, or who had given military help to the Dutch, would not be sent back to their Portuguese owners. But Johan Maurits and the Supreme Council of New Holland (as Dutch Brazil was officially known) soon had to acknowledge that without African slave labour there was no economic foundation for the further development of the colony. As late as the early 1630s the Directors of the WIC had their doubts whether participation in the slave trade and instituting

---

[59] Boxer, *De Nederlanders in Brazilië*, pp. 74-5.

slave labour were acceptable from a Christian point of view. But some years later most Calvinist ministers — although there were exceptions — declared that it was acceptable if certain conditions were fulfilled, including reasonable living conditions and conversion of the slaves to Christianity.[60] Forcing indigenous Brazilians to work as slaves was strictly forbidden in Dutch Brazil, even if this prohibition was not always respected. A policy of large-scale European immigration — the ideal of the more enthusiastic colonisers including Johan Maurits himself — was bound to fail for various reasons. It thus seemed that there was no other way but to continue and extend the Portuguese policy of working the sugar estates and other branches of the colonial economy with African slave labour. This meant that the Dutch could only expect limited support from black Brazilians.

Peculiarities of Dutch Brazil

In 1639 violent confrontations between Portuguese and Dutch were flaring up again, with guerilla bands on the Portuguese side organising terror in Pernambuco and the Dutch retaliating in kind. Both sides refused to make prisoners, and the war became bloody with lots of civilian casualties. In this situation, the role and significance of indigenous and black allied fighters could only increase for either side. The Portuguese military commander André Vidal de Negreiros, assisted by Camarão with his indigenous and Henrique Dias with his black fighters, faced the Dutch with their own indigenous allies, who knew that the Portuguese would kill all prisoners and therefore fought with great tenacity and loyalty. At the beginning of 1641 a Dutch delegation went to Bahia to negotiate with the Portuguese on making the war less inhuman by at least giving quarter to all unarmed men and women, 'regardless of status, race or colour, and including Indians, mulattos, and Negroes'. When the events surrounding the Portuguese Restoration in late 1640 became known in Brazil, the armed conflict died down for some time. The Portuguese began to remember they actually hated the Spanish

---

[60] Ibid., pp. 94-9, 107-8, 111.

even more than the Dutch, and Johan Maurits actually celebrated the Restoration in Recife and the new Dutch residence Mauritsstad. The vicious animosity between the Spanish and Portuguese was illustrated, among other things, by the Spanish custom of associating things Portuguese with things Jewish and their use of rather negative language equating the two. In 1630 this had induced the administrator of the bishopric of Rio de Janeiro to submit a request to the Spanish Crown expressing his indignation about this insulting phenomenon. The Dutch and the Portuguese tended to insult each other too, with a respectable man like António Vieira declaring in Bahia in 1640 that the Dutch were a 'depraved and apostate people'. This statement was made even before the occupation of Luanda by Johan Maurits in 1641, a rather cynical act when seen against the backdrop of his recent friendly gestures to the Portuguese. The African slave-trading city of Luanda in Portuguese Angola was to supply Dutch Brazil with new contingents of slave labour.[61]

Measures like religious toleration — Father Calado could even celebrate mass in Johan Maurits' own residence for the sake of the latter's Catholic servants — or the institution of local councils where the *moradores* could express their grievances and law courts where they could use their own language, proved not enough to conciliate the Portuguese. The historian Boxer is probably right in observing that the religious divide remained the main problem preventing acceptance of the Dutch regime by the Catholic Portuguese, even if it was also a question of social, cultural, psychological, and national differences. The Calvinist hard-liners were only one aspect of the problem because there were also hard-liners on the Catholic side. Yet even a man like Vicar-General Gaspar Ferreira of the Brazilian Jesuits was impressed by Johan Maurits' religious tolerance, and in 1643 Father Colombe de Nantes of the French Capuchins wrote to Rome speaking of 'the good prince Johan Maurits'.[62] The Council of

---

[61] Ibid., pp. 117-35.
[62] 'Prince' Johan Maurits' first Brazilian mistress Margarita Soler — he always remained a staunch bachelor — was actually the daughter of a former Augustinian monk from Valencia who had converted to Calvinism in France, married, and then became a Calvinist minister in Pernambuco. See Jose Antonio Gonsalves

the Reformed Church in Recife frequently complained of the freedom allowed to Catholics to celebrate their religion in public. Apart from exceptional cases, Calvinist attempts to convert the Portuguese had practically no result. The Catholic Portuguese seem to have abhorred the Calvinist religion, and the Portuguese wives of Brazilian Dutchmen—there were indeed quite a few 'mixed marriages'—made sure that if anything had to change at all, it was the Dutch husband who would become a Catholic and not the other way around.

The almost unlimited religious freedom of the Jews, in the view of some Calvinist ministers too extreme, led to Calvinist protests as well. By 1644 there were some 1,450 Jews in Dutch Brazil with synagogues in at least four cities, representing a third of all non-Portuguese freeburghers in the colony. Their critics claimed that the Jews could marry Christians, convert Christians to Judaism, ridicule the Christian religion with impunity, and so on. (In the same year, incidentally, the Supreme Council warned in a letter to the WIC Directors in the Netherlands that the Dutch habit of ridiculing the Catholic religion might lead to a Portuguese reaction.) But though by no means insignificant, the number and influence of the Jews in Dutch Brazil was often exaggerated. They were not a homogeneous community, with Jewish immigrants from the Netherlands or Portugal, Brazilian former crypto-Jews, and others (for example, Jews from Germany) constituting distinct groups. The fact that black Brazilians with their African background and indigenous groups were often left alone in religious matters as well, was not to the liking of the Brazilian Reformed Church either, and some Calvinist ministers insisted on greater efforts to convert them.

Indeed, not all Calvinist efforts remained without effect, especially as far as certain indigenous peoples were concerned. Among some of the Tupi and Tapuia tribes progress was made, confirming the old thesis that 'animists' were more susceptible to conversion to what was for them the new phenomenon of monotheism than were adherents of a rival monotheistic religion. Of course, part of the

---

de Mello, 'Vincent Joachim Soler in Dutch Brazil', in Van den Boogaart (ed.), *Johan Maurits van Nassau-Siegen 1604-1679: A Humanist Prince*, pp. 247-55.

indigenous population had already become acquainted with the Catholic faith, especially in the Jesuit-run *aldeias*, but this may not have been decisive given the tendency of indigenous Brazilians to only partially adopt Christianity and to embrace various forms of syncretism. A measure of resignation among the Dutch as to what could be achieved in terms of exercising cultural influence among the indigenous Brazilians certainly emerged. But this did not change the strategic need to show respect for their autonomy. Nevertheless, a handful of Indian leaders including Pieter Poti and others, seem to have become 'good Reformed Christians'.[63]

Perhaps the question of the Calvinist religion is not entirely insignificant when it comes to understanding the role of the indigenous population in Dutch Brazil. They may or must have understood that it was a major identity symbol of the new rulers, in a sense the radical opposite to Portuguese Catholicism. Developing new forms of syncretism, now adopting aspects of Dutch Calvinism, may have been a conscious response to the new situation of inter-European power struggle. A significant number of Calvinist preachers and others made attempts to convert indigenous peoples to the Reformed religion, and a number of carefully selected indigenous Brazilians were actually sent to the Netherlands for further education. In 1641 a Calvinist catechism in Tupi—part of a trilingual Dutch-Portuguese-Tupi publication—was printed in the city of Enkhuizen in Holland for distribution in Brazil. Indeed, even some Tapuia were educated in the Dutch Republic as part of the political-cultural offensive.[64] Although at first the Calvinists were disappointed by the results, by 1645 progress was reported despite

---

[63] Boxer, *De Nederlanders in Brazilië*, pp. 144-64, 191n14, 192n28, 203; see for the Jews Arnold Wiznitzer, *Os Judeus no Brasil Colonial* (São Paulo, 1966) and Van den Boogaart, 'De Nederlandse expansie', p. 122 for figures; Wätjen, *Das holländische Kolonialreich*, pp. 230-5 for anti-Jewish grievances and p. 259 for Tupi syncretism; Hemming, *Red Gold*, p. 297 for the argument of the (relative) failure of Calvinist and Dutch cultural influence over the indigenous population; but Schalkwijk, *The Reformed Church in Dutch Brazil*, pp. 152-67 for the Reformed mission to the Portuguese and, notably, Chapters 8-11 for different aspects of the Reformed mission among indigenous Brazilians, an investigation more detailed and more penetrating than any other on this question.

[64] Schalkwijk, *The Reformed Church in Dutch Brazil*, Chapter 11; C.R. Boxer, *The Dutch Seaborne Empire 1600-1800* (London, 1977), p. 150.

the realism and pessimism that obviously existed as well. The Tapuia were generally more resistant to European cultural influences than the Tupi. Yet their eagerness to collaborate with the Dutch against the Portuguese made some of them adopt Calvinist symbols and even a smattering of Reformed religious culture. As Boxer has written about the Dutch influence on the Tapuia and about the observations of António Vieira in Brazil:

> [T]hey still retained a strong memory and a certain liking for what they had learnt. A Portuguese Jesuit missionary visiting some Amerindian villages in the interior soon after the final expulsion of the Dutch, was horrified to find that 'many of the inhabitants were as Calvinist and Lutheran as if they had been born in England or in Germany'. Padre Antonio Vieira, S.J., and his colleagues soon eradicated such traces of Protestantism, which otherwise might perhaps have endured in the hinterland of north-east Brazil for as long as they did in Formosa.[65]

Exerting some measure of religious and political influence was facilitated by the tendency of Dutch representatives to treat indigenous Brazilians as equals, and apparently Johan Maurits — who had his own style of 'going native' at times — was delighted to be called 'brother' by tribal leaders. When he had to leave Brazil in 1644, he took a group of indigenous Brazilians with him. They gave a dancing performance in The Hague, which apparently was not appreciated by the local Calvinist ministers. Afterwards, Johan Maurits continued for years to send letters and gifts to indigenous Brazilians. It is also noteworthy that some Spaniards and Portuguese admitted that the 'northern nations' were more successful with the indigenous peoples than they were. The Franciscan Juan de Silva testified to the Council of the Indies in Spain in 1621 that the Dutch tended to behave better towards indigenous Brazilians and that the Spaniards' maltreatment of them had enabled the Dutch to penetrate South America, especially the Amazon and Orinoco regions and the Guyanas. Indeed, the Dutch had told indigenous groups that not the Protestants but the Catholic Spanish were 'heretics' from a Christian point of view, because 'they were breaking God's

---

[65] Boxer, *The Dutch Seaborne Empire*, p. 150. Formosa indeed was another example of a relatively successful Dutch Reformed missionary activity among the native (non-Chinese) population.

laws by their evil deeds' committed against indigenous Brazilians. António Vieira had to admit in 1654 that the Amazon peoples hated the Portuguese but entertained peaceful trade relations with the English and the Dutch, 'who respected their freedom'. A few years later he visited the isolated region in western Ceará known as the Serra de Ibiapaba where many indigenous Brazilians had fled after the collapse of Dutch Brazil. Some of them were dressed in Dutch clothes and had Dutch books, which according to Vieira they could read. In addition to his comments quoted above, he described the region as having been transformed by these 'Protestant Indians' into 'a local Geneva'. The Jesuits' opposition to the 'Indian policy' of the Portuguese colonists in Maranhão and other parts of northern Brazil eventually led to their expulsion from the region in 1684.[66]

The Reformed Church also made an (apparently much weaker) effort to bring the Calvinist religion to the black slaves. More than 23,000 Africans were imported by the Dutch to Brazil during the period 1636-1645, the beginnings of the Dutch slave trade and colonial slave-labour system, which essentially was a continuation of that of the Portuguese. Although the issue of the conversion of the slaves was frequently discussed by the Reformed Church Council at Recife, few practical steps seem to have been made. This was probably because neither the slave owners nor the Dutch administration were very enthusiastic. Especially during the first ten years of Dutch Brazil, policy on slaves was rather contradictory, and during the war years until 1641 large numbers of slaves who were fighting on the Dutch side were manumitted; the Portuguese did the same thing. But over the course of the 1640s the system of Brazilian slave labour was reconsolidated, now supported by the Dutch as well, and as a result slaves began to escape in

---

[66] Boxer, *De Nederlanders in Brazilië*, pp. 165-8, 188; Boxer, *The Dutch Seaborne Empire*, p. 150; C.R. Boxer, *A Great Luso-Brazilian Figure: Padre António Vieira, S.J., 1608-1697* (London, 1957), p. 20 where the Jesuits are described as the only Catholic religious order in Brazil with 'a long tradition of upholding the freedom' of indigenous Brazilians; see further Wätjen, *Das holländische Kolonialreich*, pp. 254-60; Fausto, *A Concise History of Brazil*, p. 46; Hemming, *Red Gold*, Chapter 15 on António Vieira and Brazil.

growing numbers. Some of their runaway settlements (*quilombos*) were destroyed by Dutch soldiers and their indigenous allies, tragic evidence that the latter did not necessarily sympathise with the black slaves but rather had their own vision of their place in Brazilian society and of the proper basis of relations between the different groups. When in 1645 a large-scale uprising broke out, of the Pernambuco Portuguese and their allies it was particularly the indigenous peoples of the northern captaincies (Itamaracá, Paraíba, Rio Grande, Ceará) that proved important allies for the Dutch, helping them to hold on to at least a part of north-east Brazil. The sugar-growing area of Pernambuco was lost by the Dutch after August 1645, and it was a bad sign for them that the uprising was supported by numbers of pro-Portuguese mixed-race, black, and indigenous Brazilians. Had the Portuguese learnt to manage these non-Europeans in a more clever way? The *mulatto* leader João Fernandes Vieira, born in Madeira, is often credited with having started the uprising even though he was probably driven by opportunistic motives. He had become an estate owner under the Dutch regime, but was indebted to Dutch and Jewish merchants. The first to join him were 150 black and mixed-race fighters led by the consistently pro-Portuguese Henrique Dias, followed not long after by the indigenous soldiers of the Catholic and pro-Portuguese veteran Camarão. Martím Soares Moreno with his indigenous fighters and the Portuguese military commander André Vidal de Negreiros joined the rebels as well. A feature of the fighting in 1645 was that a group of slaves on the Portuguese side played a crucial role in turning the tables on the Dutch in a major battle.[67]

A chaotic unravelling

In August 1645 indeed, the battle at Monte das Tabocas in Pernambuco pitted a thousand fighters on the Dutch side (including 300 indigenous soldiers) against another thousand on the Portuguese

---

[67] Boxer, *De Nederlanders in Brazilië*, pp. 169-75, 202-6; Wätjen, *Das holländische Kolonialreich*, pp. 260-1 on the black slaves; Schalkwijk, *The Reformed Church in Dutch Brazil*, p. 151 on the mission among the blacks; Hemming, *Red Gold*, pp. 299-301 on the remarkable fighter Camarão.

side. According to popular accounts, the latter were almost defeated when at the critical moment J.F. Vieira promised freedom to a group of black slaves fighting under his command if they managed to halt the Dutch attack, which they succeeded in doing. It was the incredible toughness of these West African slaves which not only prevented defeat but ensured final victory to the Portuguese and Luso-Brazilians. Other events also caused serious problems for the Dutch. In Rio Grande do Norte a number of Portuguese *moradores* were killed by Tapuia fighters led by Jacob Rabe, who, though originally from Germany, had become a Dutch agent with the indigenous tribes and was married to a Tapuia woman. In later years Rabe was referred to as a 'German Jew', but it is not certain that he was Jewish even if his name would have suggested this (the historian Arnold Wiznitzer has expressed his doubts about Rabe's Jewish identity). However this may be, in 1646 Rabe was shot dead by a Dutch army officer married to a Portuguese woman, some of whose relatives had been killed in the Rio Grande 'massacre'. The murder of the popular Rabe led to a temporary withdrawal of Tapuia support for the Dutch, which badly affected their position in the area. It became clear that the attitudes of non-European groups and 'multicultural complications' on either side could have grave consequences for the effectiveness of political and military coalitions.

These dynamics led to bloody warfare and unexpected developments, with Dutch civilians massacred to avenge the Portuguese *moradores*, and Dutch army officers married to Portuguese women deserting to the other side (the Brazilian Vanderley family are descendants of one of them). While indigenous fighters on the Dutch side captured by the Portuguese were executed without mercy, the Tapuia in their turn killed as many Portuguese as possible. The Jews were increasingly nervous too, believing that a Portuguese victory would mean their physical destruction, an anxiety that would grow in the years to come. After the Portuguese occupation of Penedo in the south of Dutch Brazil in 1645, a number of 'New Christians' accused of practising Jewish rites were arrested and sent to Lisbon to be tried by the Inquisition. Since most of them could prove they were Dutch subjects and the Portuguese-Jewish community in Amsterdam successfully pressed the Dutch government to demand their release, all but three were set free. Another case attracting much attention was that of Isaac de Castro (José de Lis), a Portuguese 'New Christian' who had gone to Dutch Brazil in 1641 and three years later to Bahia. After being denounced by people who said they had seen him visit a synagogue in Recife, he was arrested and sent to Portugal eventually to be executed in 1647 after being put on trial by the Inquisition. The prominent rabbi Isaac Aboab da Fonseca in Recife, meanwhile, vehemently attacked the 'treacherous' rebel J.F. Vieira, who was also criticised by *moradores* who claimed he took part in the uprising only because of his debts to the Dutch, not from patriotic or religious motives.[68]

Thus, the situation in north-east Brazil became ever more tense, unpredictable, and confusing. It is revealing that each side tried to persuade the other's indigenous allies to join them. Highly fascinating in this regard is an exchange from October 1645 in the Tupi language between two acculturated Potiguar leaders, one on the Portuguese, the other on the Dutch side. The pro-Portuguese Felipe Camarão (who used a scribe to write his letters) and Pieter Poti were actually cousins. Poti argued that the Dutch treated the indigenous Brazilians better than the Portuguese did and that they lived more freely under the Dutch, who had never enslaved the indigenous population and even called them 'brothers', quite unlike 'the Portuguese rascals'. There was also a religious, Protestant versus Catholic argument. Poti blamed Camarão for calling him a 'heretic' and claimed: 'I am a better Christian than you. I believe only in Christ without polluting religion with idolatry as you do in yours. I learned the Christian religion and practise it daily...' Poti had been educated in Holland and also believed that Dutch naval power would prevail. While Camarão remained loyal to the Catholic Portuguese — as did a fairly large number of Pernambuco Tupi who had left the region together with the withdrawing Luso-Brazilian forces in 1635 — another section of the Tupi had taken the side

---

[68] Boxer, *De Nederlanders in Brazilië*, pp. 207-12, 220-1; Hemming, *Red Gold*, pp. 303-4, 307-8 with his own version of the Rabe story; Wiznitzer, *Os Judeus no Brasil Colonial*, pp. 91, 97-104, 149-51; Cabral de Mello, *De Braziliaanse affaire*, pp. 88, 193n17.

of the Calvinist Dutch. In addition, most of the Tapuia tribes in the north-east remained loyal to the Dutch as well, despite the killing of Rabe and other incidents.

However, by 1648 the Dutch position in what remained of New Holland had become increasingly hopeless, especially in Pernambuco and the northern-most captaincies, now that the Portuguese military forces had come to represent a renewed coalition of European, black, and indigenous units. In 1649 a Dutch counterattack failed, and Pieter Poti was captured by the enemy. Although he was badly maltreated, he refused to disavow his Dutch allies or the Calvinist religion; he was brought in chains to Portugal but died on the way. His fate was later described in a remarkable appeal-cum-memorandum (known as the *Two Remonstrances*) presented in Holland by the indigenous leader Antonio Paräupába, a close friend of Poti and 'Regidoor' (captain) of the Rio Grande Tupi. The memorandum was published in The Hague in 1657.[69]

A Dutch report on the 1649 defeat admitted that among the enemy forces there were many 'Brazilians [Tupi], Tapuyas, Negroes, Mameluks [mestizos]'. Many of them were good guerrilla fighters and dangerous enemies; to make things worse, it was difficult to prevent Henrique Dias' black soldiers from killing Dutch prisoners of war. In 1649 the Dutch admiral Witte de With claimed that the Tapuia and Potiguar allies were losing patience with the way they were treated by the Dutch. Apparently, especially in a situation of retreat not all was well with the relationship between the Dutch and their indigenous allies. Nevertheless, many of the latter remained loyal till the end and some of them were present in besieged Recife. By 1652 the mood among the Supreme Council in Recife had become not only desperate but vicious. In a letter to WIC headquarters, the council referred to Portugal as 'the most idolatrous Catholic country' in the world. If Brazil were to be kept by the Dutch, then in future there should be 'no religious freedom' for the Portuguese, 'who have a natural antipathy against every other

---

[69] Hemming, *Red Gold*, pp. 309-11 for the Poti-Camarão correspondence and pp. 314-6 for the capture of Poti and the Paräupába memorandum; the bibliography in Boxer, *De Nederlanders in Brazilië*, contains the full title of the Paräupába memorandum: *Twee verscheyden Remonstrantien* ...

nation with a different way of life'. Obviously, these Dutchmen saw their own nation as superior to the Portuguese as far as open-mindedness and 'multicultural' toleration was concerned. But when Recife finally surrendered in 1654, the Portuguese commander Barreto not only managed to keep discipline among his troops—described by a Dutch observer as consisting of 'Whites, Mulattos, Brazilians, Negroes and Tapuyas'—but also issued the 'Capitulation of Taborda', which stipulated that the Jews were allowed to stay if they wished. However, it would seem that not a single Jew decided to do so, even though in Recife, at least, they were not maltreated. Most of them went to the Dutch Republic, while a smaller number removed to the West Indies, New Amsterdam (New York), or France.[70]

The Tapuia and Potiguar allies blamed the Dutch in bitter words for the military collapse and abandonment of their settlements in Brazil and for abandoning them to the revenge of the Portuguese. A letter from a Dutch official described how more than 4,000 indigenous Brazilians (apparently mainly Tapuias) fled from the north-eastern captaincies to seek refuge in western Ceará in the Ibiapaba hills (probably the place where Antonio Vieira found them some years later) cursing the 'Flemings' for what they saw as their lack of courage to fight on. Here they founded a 'republic' called Cambressive, from where they sent António Paräupába to the Netherlands in another attempt to obtain Dutch support. He submitted his appeal to the States General twice, in 1654 and 1656, asking for help against 'the cruel and bloodthirsty Portuguese, who since the first occupation of Brazil have destroyed so many hundreds of thousands of persons of that [Indian] nation...' Paräupába—who appears to have had a clear 'anti-colonial' consciousness—was met with sympathy, but hardly more than that. The Luso-Brazilian victors, meanwhile, had seriously begun to quarrel among themselves. Apparently, the mixed-race, black, and indigenous Brazilians who had done the toughest fighting on the

---

[70] Boxer, *De Nederlanders in Brazilië*, pp. 224-5, 235-6, 258-61, 268, 273, 277, 280-1, 287-8 for the most crucial events of the last years of Dutch Brazil; also Van den Boogaart, 'De Nederlandse expansie', pp. 124-5.

Portuguese side felt insulted by the treatment they received afterwards, and now they were ready to revolt against their masters. This also appears from a letter written to Lisbon in 1655 by J.F. Vieira, who already in 1652 had stressed the need 'to treat the Negroes, Indians and other people well who sustain the war with their lives'.[71] The building of a broader 'Pernambuco nationalism' or multiracial coalition may have been problematical from the start, even if there were early Portuguese promises in connection with the active participation of 'non-white' people in the movement for Pernambuco 'restoration'. It became even more problematical when such promises were not kept.

Concluding observations

Was the Portuguese colonial regime in north-east Brazil forced by the new circumstances resulting from the Dutch invasion to make concessions to demands for greater equality and cultural tolerance from non-European ethnic groups? Was it the more liberal policies of the Dutch regime or simply the fact that a rival power had appeared on the scene that forced the Portuguese to make at least certain promises to that effect? Were the Jews excepted from these promises? These questions are not easy to answer but, insofar as there is some evidence in the affirmative, we may speak — in a contextually circumscribed and historically relative sense — of the existence of 'decolonising' or 'de-hegemonising' tendencies. This is possible because the power of colonial regimes was never absolute and always contested, especially when new factors entered the equation. The history of seventeenth-century Brazil and the struggle between the Portuguese and the Dutch, this crisis of European power politics, colonial hegemony, and structures of social and cultural stratification cannot be properly understood without considering the critical role played by different indigenous and other non-European or non-white populations. During the relatively short but fascinating period of 1624-54 all Brazilian actors — including the

---

[71] Boxer, *De Nederlanders in Brazilië*, pp. 290, 300; Hemming, *Red Gold*, pp. 315-6, 619 referring for the Paräupába appeal also to Souto Maior, 'Fastos Pernambucanos'.

Dutch, the Jews, and others who eventually were losers in the power struggle — were part of the same colonial drama. Each group played its role and defined its interests in its own unique way, not only in terms of political or economic interests but also in terms of social status, cultural and religious identity, and even colonial ideology. For a certain period of time the situation in north-east Brazil was relatively open-ended as far as patterns of colonial domination and stratification were concerned, including the status of 'free' or 'half-free' indigenous and other subaltern groups such as free black and mixed-race Brazilians or even African slaves. We must take care not to fall into the trap of anachronistic judgements and generalisations, in particular the supposition that no meaningful change was possible in the power structure of Brazilian society and the status of subordinate groups — with indigenous Brazilians and people of African descent bound to be eternal victims and Catholic Portuguese unchallenged colonial masters. It was not preordained that Brazil should be a strictly hierarchical and culturally rigid, intolerant society.

Both for opportunistic and for moral, 'idealistic', or religious reasons, a degree of 'multicultural toleration' and socio-political fairness was envisaged by at least some in seventeenth-century Brazil. Perhaps it is true that this tendency existed especially among a minority of the Dutch invaders including more educated and liberal people like Johan Maurits of Nassau, for whom the idea and experience of religious toleration or cultural diversity were more acceptable than for the more 'monolithic' Catholic Portuguese. But of course even the seventeenth-century Catholic world had its internal debates and disagreements, as was illustrated by men like António Vieira and other critical Jesuits, Franciscans, and others. More broad-minded Catholics and liberal Calvinists alike advocated enlightened policies in complicated 'multicultural' and colonial situations. At the same time, a more egalitarian, pragmatic, or even 'syncretic' attitude that would help to protect different modes of life and interethnic co-existence was also part of the mind-set of indigenous Brazilians. Among Lusophone free black and mixed-race Brazilians, visions of a more egalitarian order existed as well, as became apparent in the later 1640s and 1650s, while among black slaves resistance in the form of flight but also occasional demands for emancipation were part of the colonial situation.

This complex clash of different visions, options, and strategies must surely be a subject of further historical research, and should also inform 'post-colonial' debates on the legacy of colonialism. The crises of colonial Brazil, of which the seventeenth-century Dutch invasion was arguably but one, and the 'decolonising potential' that was almost always there as a perspective for change have perhaps not been fully examined. At the end of the day, the indigenous peoples were the major victims of the course of Brazilian history — the victimisation of Africans was even worse in some but less hopeless in other respects. However, for a long time they were active participants in this history, playing their own political and military role, developing their own cultural initiatives (notably religious syncretism and expressing ambivalent attitudes to Christianity), and articulating their own aspirations in the colonial context.

John Hemming has written that the tragedy of the 'Indians' was that 'they were being armed and incited against one another by colonial powers ... Not only did traditionally hostile groups fight one another, but also tribes normally as cohesive as the Potiguar were violently split by the rival European colonists and religions.'[72] This is undoubtedly part of the truth, and yet various indigenous groups — or their chiefs and more acculturated leaders — must be given credit for their ability to make their own rational and strategic choices. This ability was revealed — but of course not only then — during the crisis triggered by the creation of 'Dutch Brazil', when a serious destabilisation of the colonial order opened new opportunities for resistance and autonomy among the indigenous population, for a re-arrangement of interethnic and multicultural patterns, and even for a form of 'partial' or 'relative decolonisation' through the removal of Portuguese colonial power by another (perhaps temporarily more 'tolerant') colonial power. This was, of course, an exercise in re-colonisation above all else, but by putting in place some new political, social, and cultural patterns it also held the promise of 'de-hegemonising' certain dimensions of Brazilian

---

[72] Hemming, *Red Gold*, p. 309.

society. For several groups of indigenous Brazilians, for 'New Christians' and Jews, even for some Catholic friars, and perhaps for others, there must have been reasons to support the new colonial power that seemed prepared to respect their freedom more than the Portuguese had done. Of this strange episode in Portuguese and Brazilian history, the miraculous 'Maurício' was the symbol.

6. Portugal, Slovakia and the political Counter-Reformation of the twentieth century (1910-1939)

This essay presents a comparative analysis of the political dynamics of Portugal and Slovakia in the first half of the twentieth century (1910-1939), focussing on the significance of conservative political Catholicism. The two countries belonged to a group of European nations in which there was a strong reaction to political liberalism, progressive republicanism, cultural secularism, and socialism. This antagonism can arguably be seen as a modern continuation of the historic conflict between the Protestant and humanist Reformation on one side, and the Catholic Counter-Reformation on the other. Its twentieth-century manifestation was of course somewhat different from the original sixteenth- and seventeenth-century conflict. After the eighteenth century, the historic force of anti-Catholic Reformation was mainly expressed in the form of intellectual Enlightenment, anti-clericalism, and social and cultural progressivism. But in many ways, the dynamics and aggressive energy of this great cultural confrontation continued during the nineteenth and twentieth centuries, although in a modified ideological and political shape. Between 1910 and 1940 the conflict between political progressivism and Catholic conservatism reached its culmination. In Portugal the forces of cultural secularism and liberal republicanism were defeated by the new authoritarian regime led by Salazar. In Slovakia the foundation and then the end of the First Czechoslovak Republic brought the rise and victory of the Catholic opposition movement, the Slovak People's Party of Andrej Hlinka and Jozef Tiso. The authors of this essay would argue that a comparison of Portugal and Slovakia sheds light on the significance of the political force of conservative and anti-liberal Catholicism. From a Slovak point of view, looking at Portugal seems helpful in coming to terms with this European and Slovak phenomenon.

Introduction

The Reformation of the sixteenth century was a major force in European history, but so was the Counter-Reformation of the late sixteenth and seventeenth centuries. The 'dialectical dynamics' of the two tendencies continued during the eighteenth and even the nineteenth and twentieth centuries. The age of Enlightenment, secularisation, and the rise of modern political movements saw an ongoing struggle between these antagonistic spiritual, cultural, and social movements even if secularisation and modernisation changed the terms of their confrontation to some extent.

How should we define 'Reformation' in this wider historical, political, and cultural sense? And how 'Counter-Reformation'? The Reformation was a cultural revolution in Europe which paved the way for a more autonomous and educated civil society in various countries of the continent. The struggle for the emancipation of European citizens and middle- and lower-class groups continued through the twentieth century. The struggle for the acceptance of critical thought, more democratic and liberal institutions, and political and social emancipation was not always an easy one in Protestant societies either. But it is probably true that, generally speaking, in European (and American) Protestant societies more progress was made in this regard than in Catholic societies, although some Catholic regions proved considerably less conservative than others. Broadly speaking, the Counter-Reformation was a cultural and political movement to fight back against the advance of liberal individualism, civic emancipation, and secular political thought. The old values of religious tradition, social hierarchy, and political and cultural conservatism were to be defended against the onslaught of political and societal fragmentation. In what follows we will define 'political Counter-Reformation' as the reaction of conservative Catholicism to political progressivism, liberalism, republicanism, and cultural secularism. While we are focusing on conservative Catholicism, it should be realised that there was also another, more modern and more democratic form of political Catholicism: Christian Democracy in various European countries including Germany, the Benelux countries, and even Italy. Finally,

Catholic conservatism was not the only form of conservatism: there was also a Protestant, an Orthodox, a nationalist, and even a liberal variant of conservatism. But here we are specifically concerned with Catholic conservatism in some of its national political manifestations, namely in Portugal and Slovakia. While there were interesting similarities between the two cases, there were also differences between them regarding the type of political regime in the 1930s and of political programmes as formulated by the forces of Catholic opposition before that crucial decade.

Both Portugal and Slovakia belonged to the 'backward zone' of Europe in terms of Catholic conservative domination and backlash against liberal middle-class culture and society. Slovakia had actually experienced the victory of the Lutheran Reformation in the sixteenth and much of the seventeenth century; in other parts of the old Hungarian Kingdom Calvinism had been triumphant. But after the late seventeenth century, the Catholic and Habsburg cultural regime had been restored, although a Lutheran minority survived in parts of Slovakia. In Portugal there had never been a successful Reformation, but during the first half of the sixteenth century Renaissance humanism had reached a high cultural and intellectual level, which afterwards was largely suppressed by the forces of Counter-Reformation and the Inquisition. Nevertheless, in the eighteenth and nineteenth centuries enlightened and secularising political and cultural tendencies emerged, which seemed to set Portugal on a new course. In many ways, this development reached its culmination in the Portuguese First Republic of 1910-26. But then the coming to power of Salazar and the rise of an increasingly fascist regime consolidated the 'political neo-Counter-Reformation' for a long time to come.

In Slovakia the political force of conservative Catholic nationalism (the political movement led by Andrej Hlinka from the early years of the twentieth century) began to attack the liberal and progressive Czechoslovak government soon after the foundation of the Czechoslovak Republic in 1918. The movement's criticism of Czechoslovak national policy was often legitimate, but its oppositional attitude was much more than that and also embraced a fundamental cultural critique. The Hlinka movement—the autonomist

Slovak People's Party—became the strongest political force in Slovakia in the 1920s and 1930s. Its agitation was partly aimed at the 'Hussite' (for them a term of abuse) cultural, religious, and educational policies of the Prague government, in particular the government's attempts to restrict the power and influence of the Catholic Church in Slovak public, political, and cultural life. Both in Slovakia and Portugal the struggle of the political Counter-Reformation against the endeavours of 'neo-Reformist' or anti-clerical secularism, liberal individualism, and progressive republicanism, and against reduction of the Catholic Church to a more marginal and private position in politics and society, carried on relentlessly. In Portugal this finally resulted in the dictatorship of Salazar and the *Estado Novo* in the early 1930s, in Slovakia in the institution of an autonomist regime in October 1938 and the pro-German Slovak State led by Jozef Tiso some five months later.

Both cases were examples of the ongoing dynamics of the—broadly defined—long-term Counter-Reformation in its twentieth-century political expression. The Counter-Reformation assumed a more modern face, i.e. the shape of a modern political movement or an anti-democratic political regime. It is true that in some parts of Europe there was also another form of political Catholicism: modern Christian Democracy in countries like Germany, Belgium, The Netherlands, Italy, and even Austria (an ambivalent case) and the Czech Lands (especially Moravia).[73] However, Slovakia and Portugal (along with several other countries including Spain, France, and Hungary) represented significant cases of European countries where Counter-Reformation or indeed 'Neo-Inquisition' (a term coined by Antonio de Figueiredo) traditions and regimes managed to consolidate a long-lasting conservative Catholic domination.

---

[73] See for example the essays in Lex Heerma van Voss, Patrick Pasture, and Jan De Maeyer (eds.), *Between Cross and Class: Comparative Histories of Christian Labour in Europe 1840-2000* (Bern, 2005). In this work both political-ideological and organised-labour aspects of the 'Catholic alternative' to socialism and liberalism are discussed and analysed.

Portugal

The Catholic tradition among the peasantry and common people of Portugal was widely seen as naïve, primitive, and open to manipulation. According to Antonio de Figueiredo, a rather anti-clerical author who was born in 1929, the religion of Portuguese peasants, 'which is supposed to be Catholicism, is a form of sub-Christianity, for in their simple minds instead of love there is a superstitious fear of a God of Terror. The local priest, like a tribal witchdoctor, teaches them a doctrine which holds that challenges to the local and national patron saints can be punished with crop failure or the affliction of their animals and children.'[74] The urban middle classes were of a somewhat different type and had been the social basis of a liberal constitutional, anti-clerical, and even a radical republican movement against the monarchy and the power of the Catholic Church. The republican and secularist agitation at the time of the nineteenth-century constitutional monarchy intensified during the early years of the twentieth century and made the continuation of the monarchical order increasingly difficult. While a democratic republic was favoured by some, others saw a socially protective authoritarian regime as an alternative to the dysfunctional monarchy. In 1907-8 the dictator João Franco tried to introduce social reforms to help stabilise the monarchical order after parliamentary rule had been suspended. But in February 1908 the Portuguese king, Carlos I, and the heir to the throne were murdered by two republican revolutionaries. Conservative Catholics, including the young António de Oliveira Salazar (1889-1970), were shocked and grew increasingly anxious. Salazar was destined to become the leader of an anti-liberal and Counter-Reformation regime whose origins can be traced back to the political crisis of the early years of the twentieth century. In 1908 Salazar ended his studies at the Seminary of Viseu without proceeding to the priesthood. He acquired the qualifications necessary to enter the Faculty of Law and moved to the University of Coimbra in 1910, where he and other Portuguese

---

[74] Antonio de Figueiredo, *Portugal: Fifty Years of Dictatorship* (Harmondsworth, 1975), p. 11.

Catholics were to witness the end of the monarchy itself, as well as the threat of a series of frightening political, social, and cultural changes. On 5 October 1910, indeed, the Republic was proclaimed, with the new Portuguese king, Manuel II, fleeing to London.[75]

The coup d'état of October 1910, a Lisbon urban revolution, was triggered off by a group of junior military officers influenced by republican ideology. The Portuguese republican movement was largely a movement of the professional classes, intellectuals, freemasons, junior army officers (including a group of secretive 'carbonari'), and anti-clericalists. The greatest republican leader, Afonso Costa, became minister of justice of the Provisional Government and began to curtail religious privileges, which included the banning of clerical dress outside of churches, dissolving monasteries, forcing many parish priests to retire, exiling bishops, and encouraging the growth of masonic lodges. On 8 October 1910 a decree was promulgated by the republican government to curb the activities of the Jesuits and other religious orders. Ten days later the religious oath was abolished; on 22 October Catholic teaching in schools was prohibited; and the next day the Faculty of Theology of the University of Coimbra was closed down. On 26 October 1910 twenty-six holy days became working days. On 3 November divorce was legally established and shortly afterwards the marriage ceremony became a civil function. These measures were seen by traditional Catholics as 'equivalent to free love' or worse. A Law of Separation of Church and State was being planned whereby Catholicism would cease to be the established religion of Portugal. Under this law all ecclesiastical property would be claimed by the State.[76] But the ambitious programme of the first republican governments on these and other matters soon led to sharp disagreements between different political figures and different parties,

---

[75] Figueiredo, *Portugal*, pp. 23-5; David Birmingham, *A Concise History of Portugal*, 2nd ed. (Cambridge, 2003), p. 148; Hugh Kay, *Salazar and Modern Portugal* (New York, 1970), pp. 10-12; Filipe Ribeiro De Meneses, *Salazar: A Political Biography* (New York, 2009), pp. 12-3.

[76] Birmingham, *A Concise History of Portugal*, pp. 148-53, 159; Figueiredo, *Portugal*, pp. 26-7; for the 'religious question' Vítor Neto, 'A questão religiosa: Estado, Igreja e conflitualidade sócio-religiosa', in Fernando Rosas and Maria Fernanda Rollo (eds.), *História da Primeira República Portuguesa* (Lisbon, 2010), pp. 129-48.

including the Republican Party, the more radical Democratic Party, and the Evolutionist Party, the latter being more moderate or even right-wing. Lay education, divorce, separation of Church and State, limitation of religious orders, and expulsion of monks and nuns were controversial among the republicans themselves, especially as far as the manner and degree of their practical implementation was concerned. Salazar, for his part, always remembered the agitation against the Church and its dangerous consequences.[77] Not only anti-clerical policy itself, but in particular the political and ideological agitation surrounding it, was a danger Salazar and like-minded spirits wished to bring under control in a future post-republican and post-liberal era.

The anti-clerical offensive against the traditional position of the Catholic Church involved not only ideological and political agitation by various political parties, freemasons, and others, but also, sometimes, physical violence. During Salazar's years in Coimbra after 1910, he and his Catholic fellow students used to go to the Church of St John to attend the 'Month of Mary' ceremonies with *mocas* (clubs) under their cloaks to defend themselves against their anti-clerical adversaries.[78] Part of the students at Coimbra University, indeed, were expressing their sympathy for the Republic in sometimes violent or destructive ways. But on the other side were the more conservative students, organised in the Catholic study group *Centro Academico de Democracia Cristã* (CADC), which had been founded in 1901 and temporarily banned by the republican regime. Many of the CADC members looked to the idealised past and hoped to restore an absolutist monarchy. They also had ideas about social and political reforms and, increasingly, about a new type of authoritarian regime as an anti-liberal and Catholic alternative. Under the editorship of Manuel Gonçalves Cerejeira, who later, during the rule of Salazar, was to become Cardinal Patriarch of Lisbon, the CADC published a weekly magazine, *O Imparcial*. Perhaps this name expressed their belief that their views were above the false, subjective, or superficial opinions of others. By 1919

---

[77] Figueiredo, *Portugal*, pp. 48-50; Meneses, *Salazar*, p. 14.
[78] Kay, *Salazar and Modern Portugal*, p. 26; Figueiredo, *Portugal*, p. 30.

the Catholic students around the Coimbra magazine had become a rather cohesive group of ideologists.

The young Portuguese Catholic, monarchist, and conservative thinkers were studying such socio-political guides as Pope Leo XIII's encyclical *Rerum Novarum* (1891), but also the works of prominent French right-wing writers and reactionary ideologists such as Charles Maurras. These doctrines offered 'organic' and hierarchical concepts that could be seen as a continuation of the 'corporate' character of medieval and ancient regime society, and as an alternative to the 'excessive' egalitarianism and individualism of the French revolution, liberal parliamentary democracy, republican secularism, atheism, and Marxist internationalism. Some of these ideas were adapted to Portuguese conditions by the traditionalist writer Antonio Sardinha and others who promoted the nationalist doctrine known as 'Lusitanian integralism'. This Portuguese variant of Maurras's integral nationalism was rather spiritualist, sentimental, and romanticising but also based on elitist concepts and an aversion to social change—thus combining ideas which had the potential to develop into a fascist world view. However, it is also true that Salazar and others tended to delimit their Catholic conservatism and anti-liberal authoritarianism from the new fascism of the 1920s, whose pagan, extremist, and violent political practices and ideology they rejected.[79]

---

[79] Figueiredo, *Portugal*, pp. 27-8; Birmingham, *A Concise History of Portugal*, p. 160. See for the integralist movement of the monarchist right, in many ways the Portuguese equivalent of Maurras's *Action Française*, Carlos Ferrão, *O Integralismo e a República*, 2 vols. (Lisbon, 1964-5); Rivera Martins de Carvalho, *O Pensamento integralista perante o Estado Novo* (Lisbon, 1971). See for some relevant observations on Maurras, conservative Catholic thought, and the ideological link with fascism, Edward R. Tannenbaum, *The Action Française* (New York, 1962); F.L. Carsten, *The Rise of Fascism* (Berkeley and Los Angeles, 1967), pp. 13-17; Juan J. Linz, 'Some Notes Towards a Comparative Study of Fascism in Sociological Historical Perspective', in Walter Laqueur (ed.), *Fascism: A Reader's Guide. Analyses, Interpretations, Bibliography* (Harmondsworth, 1979), pp. 13-78, here esp. p. 67n11; Stanley G. Payne, 'Fascism in Western Europe', in ibid., pp. 300-21, here esp. p. 302; Zeev Sternhell, 'Fascist Ideology', in ibid., pp. 325-406, here esp. pp. 340, 349; Eugen Weber, 'Revolution? Counter-revolution? What Revolution?', in ibid., pp. 488-531, here esp. p. 501. These authors discuss the differences and similarities between the ideas of right-wing Catholicism and those of fascism.

Over time, Salazar emerged as an important thinker, writer, and Catholic ideologist. He made contributions to the *Imparcial*, the *Revista de Estudos* — similarly connected with the CADC — and newspapers published in Lisbon and Porto. He also wrote a study on labour relations entitled 'The Peace of Christ among the Working Class', indicating a Catholic approach to the social question and a serious intention to protect the lower classes. In a 'Catholic address' he declared that it was necessary to create 'a strong Portugal, an educated Portugal, a moral Portugal, a hard-working and progressive Portugal'. In his view, the conviction that Portugal should be more 'educated' and economically developed was obviously not in conflict with conservative Catholic ideas on the need to preserve traditional social and cultural patterns. A combination of corporatism, authoritarianism with a social face, and controlled modernisation might deliver what Salazar began to see as an alternative future for Portugal. A more responsible and professional economic policy and a right-wing national revolution were to become the pillars for this — to be erected by Salazar himself. In 1914 Salazar graduated in law at the University of Coimbra as one of the best students ever. By 1917 he had become an assistant professor of economic policy and finance at the Law School. In 1918 he obtained his doctorate while already being celebrated in conservative circles as one of Portugal's 'most powerful minds' and best financial and economic experts of 'the new generation'.[80]

Salazar's political views began to crystallise. Secular republicanism, liberal democracy, and left-wing internationalism were to be rejected and to be replaced with a nationalist ideology based upon conservative religious and social principles and a glorification of Portuguese history. In 1921 Salazar was briefly a member of parliament for a Catholic party but was put off by the ruling disorder, which confirmed his conviction that 'liberal individualism' and parliamentarianism had led to the fragmentation of society and a perversion of democracy. Salazar had a nationalist vision stressing the drama of Portuguese struggle and survival — perhaps not much unlike the myth of 'the Slovak struggle for survival' that lasted for

---

[80] Kay, *Salazar and Modern Portugal*, pp. 23-4; Figueiredo, *Portugal*, pp. 29-30.

a thousand years. But while the Slovaks had to struggle as a stateless nation from the end of Great Moravia in the early tenth century to the end of Great Hungary in 1918, Portugal had continued its historic struggle for survival as an independent kingdom since the twelfth century. Salazar wrote (probably around 1920): 'Crushed in the western strip of the Peninsula, between powerful neighbours and the ocean, our existence is necessarily one long drama: but by the favour of Providence we can count eight centuries of toil and suffering, struggle and liberty, and if the danger remains, the miracle remains also...'[81] Perhaps it is true that, for Salazar and like-minded Catholic nationalists, life under the republican regime, with its less exalted views of Portugal's past and its chaotic conditions in the present, was tormenting. Yet, progressive republicans and traditionalist Catholics alike agreed on the need to awaken Portugal from its stagnation and decline. The facts were known, including the deplorable state of popular education.

In 1911 an astonishing 69.7 per cent of the Portuguese population were illiterate (60.8 per cent of men, 77.4 per cent of women). This was the case even though during the first year of the Republic (1910-1911) the number of schools had increased by 20 per cent.[82] Both Republicans and Catholic monarchists felt the need for a national revolution to improve social and cultural conditions. But they differed sharply about the ultimate goal and the nature of such a revolution and also about the causes of the national decline. The republican and left-wing political forces believed that Portugal's monarchist and Catholic past was responsible for the bad state of the country. The traditionalists, on the other hand, blamed the 'libertarian' period of the constitutional monarchy (the political liberalism and reformism since the 1820s), the irresponsible freedom of the press, and all the features of parliamentary government, which allegedly had 'carried the seeds of subversion of established social and religious values'.[83] In other words, they rejected liberal

---

[81] Figueiredo, *Portugal*, pp. 34-5; Kay, *Salazar and Modern Portugal*, p. 32.
[82] Figueiredo, *Portugal*, pp. 38-9, 51; Maria Cândida Proença, 'A educação', in Rosas and Rollo (eds.), *História da Primeira República Portuguesa*, pp. 169-89 for the general condition and controversies of education.
[83] Figueiredo, *Portugal*, p. 39.

constitutionalism, unrestricted political freedom, and the weakening of traditional Catholic values. This was identified with the main trends of almost a century of weak monarchical government that was undermined by democratic and republican tendencies.[84] Part of the Catholic conservatives proposed in effect an authoritarian alternative to restore order and confidence in Portugal's future, and to improve its overall political, economic, and cultural condition. These different aspects were closely interrelated. It is true that the republicans had inherited a humanitarian tradition from the liberals and constitutionalists under the monarchy, including — as early as 1867 — the abolition of the death penalty.[85] But the situation under the republican governments had steadily worsened because of the endemic political unrest, divisions, and instability. The truth is that Portugal's First Republic — quite in contrast to the First Czechoslovak Republic — had not become a success, neither politically nor economically. The working class was soon disillusioned by the lack of effective social reforms, and massive numbers of Portuguese peasants continued to emigrate overseas, especially to Brazil. Between 1910 and 1925 there were 518 registered strikes across the country. Salazar and the CADC were closely observing the social agitation and political turmoil, which reinforced their dislike of democratic and parliamentary rule and of the freedom of press and association. They tried to counter the chaos, indiscipline, and subversion — as they saw it — with Catholic Workers' and Youth Associations, which were linked to Christian social groups in Italy, France, and other countries.[86]

---

[84] In his analysis of nineteenth-century Portugal, David Birmingham speaks of a 'bourgeois monarchy', 'democratic royalists', 'liberal ascendancy', and so on; see Birmingham, *A Concise History of Portugal*, Chapter 5. Fernando Rosas speaks of an 'oligarchic liberalism' which dominated the last decades of the monarchy; see Fernando Rosas, 'A crise do liberalismo oligárquico em Portugal', in Rosas and Rollo (eds.), *História da Primeira República Portuguesa*, pp. 15-26.

[85] Figueiredo, *Portugal*, p. 51.

[86] Figueiredo, *Portugal*, pp. 42-3. See for the Catholic trade union and labour movements, for example, Pieter van Duin and Zuzana Poláčková, '"Against the Red Industrial Terror!": The Struggle of Christian Trade Unions in Austria and Czechoslovakia Against Socialist Trade-Union and Workplace Domination, 1918-1925', in Heerma van Voss et al. (eds.), *Between Cross and Class: Comparative*

Salazar was angered, too, by the allegedly indiscriminate arrests of different oppositional figures and groups of people during the republican period. This could be seen as proof of the Republic's weakness and insecurity but also as a threat to conservative political forces. When Salazar had to defend himself during a disciplinary inquiry at the University of Coimbra in 1919, he alleged that '...in the course of a few years, half the population of Portugal – monarchists, Catholics, democrats, Evolutionists, Camachists, syndicalists, Sidonists, and some with no political views at all – have entered the prisons and fortresses of the republic...'[87] This was an interesting summary of the various political groups and ideologies on the (broadly defined) Portuguese illiberal Right. If the monarchists, Catholics, more conservative democrats, and right-wing republican Evolutionists could all, with some good will, be counted to the Right, this was arguably also true for the National Syndicalists (an Iberian type of fascists),[88] the Sidonists (supporters of Major

---

Histories of Christian Labour in Europe 1840-2000, pp. 127-171; William Patch, 'Fascism, Catholic Corporatism, and the Christian Trade Unions of Germany, Austria, and France', in ibid., pp. 173-201.

[87] Figueiredo, *Portugal*, p. 44. See for the different anti-liberal political groups in Portugal, Ernesto Castro Leal, 'A transformação política da República: as direitas da direita antiliberal', in Rosas and Rollo (eds.), *História da Primeira República Portuguesa*, pp. 485-502. Salazar's attitude to the monarchists was complex and ambivalent. He rejected them insofar as they were opposed to the social doctrines espoused by Pope Leo XIII. Apparently, Salazar was never a true monarchist, but he gained the support of most of them even though in 1935 his regime had to suppress a monarchist revolt.

[88] The Portuguese National Syndicalists ('Blue Shirts'), re-organised by Francisco Rolão Preto in 1932, were the only genuine fascist movement in Portugal. In the 1930s they were torn between supporting the Salazar regime and denouncing it as bourgeois. After an abortive revolt in 1934 the movement was dissolved and the extremists among them were silenced. Salazar denounced them as foreign-inspired and un-Portuguese, and stressed the fundamental differences between an exalted and violent fascism and the conservative Catholic corporatism of his Estado Novo. See Kay, *Salazar and Modern Portugal*, p. 55; Howard J. Wiarda, *Corporatism and Development: The Portuguese Experience* (Amherst, MA, 1977), p. 79; Meneses, *Salazar*, pp. 126-30; Payne, 'Fascism in Western Europe', pp. 310-11; Weber, 'Revolution? Counter-revolution? What Revolution?', p. 502, arguing that Salazar established his power (like Antonescu in Romania) 'in traditional terms'. See for the Spanish National Syndicalists (Falange), Carsten, *The Rise of Fascism*, pp. 194-204.

Sidónio Pais, short-lived dictator in 1917-18),[89] and the Camachists (supporters of Brito Camacho, another increasingly right-wing republican leader and founder of the Unionist Party). Salazar was well acquainted with the complex political spectrum in Portugal and may have seen some of these groups as potential allies in a new right-wing movement. But at least as important was a new movement of Catholic resistance to republican anti-clericalism, based on claims of apparitions of the Virgin Mary in 1916-7 and leading to the cult of 'Our Lady of Fatima', which was eventually sanctioned by the Bishop of Leiria in 1930. According to the child shepherds who reported the apparition, the Virgin had announced that Portugal would soon be rescued from war and chaos by a 'saviour'. Perhaps not surprisingly, it was a member of the CADC who launched the first issue of a new periodical, *The Voice of Fatima*.[90]

A conservative revolution

There were monarchist and military revolts against the republic in 1915, 1917-8 (led by the rather popular Sidónio Pais, president-dictator for one year), 1925, and finally in 1926. The entire period of the republic was marked by violence, disunity, and instability, with political murders committed by both the Left and the Right and large numbers of strikers and protestors shot. During the period of 1910-1926 Portugal had nine presidents, forty-four governments, and twenty-five uprisings.[91] It is probably true that 'the conviction spread that only the urgent imposition of a dictatorship would

---

[89] Sidónio Pais, a former freemason and republican, was helped by trade union protests against Portugal's participation in the First World War to take power in 1917. See Birmingham, *A Concise History of Portugal*, pp. 155-6; and on the intriguing phenomenon of 'Sidonism' (a populist social authoritarianism) Maria Alice Samara, 'Sidonismo e restauração da República. Uma "encruzilhada de paixões contraditórias"', in Rosas and Rollo (eds.), *História da Primeira República Portuguesa*, pp. 371-95.
[90] Figueiredo, *Portugal*, pp. 44-7.
[91] José Hermano Saraiva, *Portugal: a companion history*, ed. by Ian Robertson and L.C. Taylor (Manchester, 1997), pp. 108-9; Figueiredo, *Portugal*, pp. 47-50, 58; Kay, *Salazar and Modern Portugal*, p. 26, who speaks of anarchy, violence, 'arbitrary imprisonment', and 'religious persecution' during the Republic; Wiarda, *Corporatism and Development*, p. 46.

restore social tranquillity and political harmony', and that the military intervention of 1926 was welcomed by many if not most classes of the population, among whom an authoritarian regime was, at least at first, generally tolerated as the belief in liberal parliamentarianism had seriously declined.[92] The coup d'état of 28 May 1926 by Catholic army officers put an end to the republic, to the political anarchy, and to the anti-Catholic agitation. 'Street power' (a term of Salazar) could now be ended and law and order imposed. According to Salazar, 'true liberty can only exist in the spirit of man... there can be absolute authority; there can never be absolute liberty; order has always been the true condition of beauty.'[93] After 1926 many — but not all — republican and anti-clerical achievements, including in part the secularisation of education, were reversed. But the clock was not turned back completely as far as the monarchy or the position of the Church was concerned, and Salazar did not come to power immediately. Even though republican protests against new legislation which facilitated the organisation of religious processions were dismissed, the monarchy was not restored and neither was the property of the Church. In 1928 General Óscar Carmona, actually a republican and freemason, became president of what gradually evolved into a new authoritarian republic supported by the army and the Church. The leader of the coup of 1926, General Gomes da Costa, had already echoed Mussolini: 'The parliamentary system has outlived its day... what we need is a real National Government which will enable the State to fulfil its mission on a basis of justice and honour. But only the army... can give the citizen liberty — safe and sane liberty of the kind he needs.'[94] However, the military dictatorship of the late 1920s remained at first rather chaotic and politically indecisive, and only when Salazar was appointed prime minister in 1932, Portugal finally acquired a leader who brought clarity and direction to the new authoritarian regime.

The time had arrived for Catholic nationalists like Salazar and similar-minded men to come to the fore. One of the youngest and

---

[92] Saraiva, *Portugal*, p. 110 for the quotation; see also Wiarda, *Corporatism and Development*, pp. 47, 81-2, 92.
[93] Quoted in Figueiredo, *Portugal*, p. 51.
[94] Ibid., p. 58 for the quotation; see also Meneses, *Salazar*, p. 64.

most remarkable right-wing enthusiasts beside Salazar himself was Marcelo Caetano, a Lisbon law student who was destined to be his successor as president and dictator after 1968. Caetano was the editor of a political magazine called the *New Order*, which in its inaugural issue proclaimed a set of principles that were even further to the right than those of the CADC, and rather hot-headed if not eccentric. Indeed, it was to be an 'anti-modern, anti-liberal, anti-democratic, anti-bourgeois, and anti-Bolshevik magazine; counter-revolutionary and reactionary; Catholic, Apostolic and Roman; monarchist, intolerant and intransigent...' Meanwhile the more experienced men of the 'integralist' movement professed the theory of 'Lusitanianism', arguing among other things that the Portuguese were racially descended from the pre-Roman tribe of the Lusitanians, who had bravely resisted the Roman occupation.[95] But it was really Salazar who was the coming man. President Carmona invited him to become minister of finance in the new cabinet in 1928, after he had been hailed by the conservative Catholic press as 'a great intellectual' and financial expert. In fact, he had already been invited by the dictator Sidónio Pais to join the finance ministry in 1918 but declined the offer while wisely waiting for more auspicious days. Ten years later Salazar described his acceptance to become finance minister as a sacrifice he was willing to make for his country. His position as a financial dictator, effectively decreed in 1928-29, became the basis for wider dictatorial powers. In 1932 Salazar became prime minister, but he continued to pretend that he did not want absolute power. In theory he remained true to what he had said at the First Eucharistic Congress in Braga in 1924: one must not 'aspire to power as a right, but accept it as a duty, considering the State as God's Ministry for the common good.'[96]

---

[95] Figueiredo, *Portugal*, p. 57.
[96] Ibid., pp. 59-64. The financial and technocratic starting-point of Salazar's dictatorship is expressed in a variety of epithets such as 'monetarist autocrat', 'technocratic dictator', 'petit-bourgeois monocrat', or 'paternalist, nationalist autocrat'. See e.g. Birmingham, *A Concise History of Portugal*, pp. 132, 164. Salazar's profile as a conservative intellectual and financial expert marked him off from other autocrats or semi-fascist leaders.

It is true that Salazar remained cautious and reticent for a long time as far as ideological statements were concerned. Only in 1939 did he dare to openly proclaim—in an English-language publication—what were his real objective and ideology: 'We are anti-parliamentarian, anti-democratic, anti-liberal, and we are determined to establish a Corporative State.'[97] The junta that came to power in 1926 did not have a clear doctrine or political programme apart from restoring law and order and suppressing democracy. This meant that Salazar had the opportunity, moving step by step, to introduce his own version of the autocratic state, underpinned by a corporatist, conservative Catholic, and nationalist ideology. In 1930, even before he became prime minister, Salazar presented the Manifesto of the National Union, which was to be Portugal's only legal political organisation.[98]

This quasi-mass movement was markedly different from a fascist mass movement in the proper sense of the term. Although Salazar became more explicitly anti-democratic, his political philosophy was rooted in an interpretation of the Catholic social doctrine, much like the authoritarian Catholic regime of Engelbert Dollfuss in Austria. The corporatist system he wanted to build was based on similar interpretations of *Rerum Novarum* and its successor *Quadragesimo anno* of Pope Pius XI (1931), which provided a blueprint for corporatist systems. In order to carry out his political project, Salazar gradually gathered his nucleus of close collaborators and national leaders. As noted above, one of them was Marcelo Caetano, who became a professor of law at Lisbon University in 1933, at the age of only twenty-seven. Caetano had written several books on legal and 'corporate' matters, and seems to have been instrumental in drafting the 1933 Constitution of the *Estado Novo* ('New State'), in theory a corporatist state representing organic interest groups rather than political parties or individuals. While the national interest was always to have priority over group interests, there was to be a Corporative Chamber in addition to a National Assembly with

---

[97] António de Oliveira Salazar, *Doctrine and Action: Internal and Foreign Policy of the New Portugal, 1928-1939* (London, 1939), p. 29.
[98] Figueiredo, *Portugal*, p. 66.

advisory powers. Portuguese corporatism and authoritarianism were in some ways similar to Italian fascism, but there were also some significant differences in terms of ideology and political culture.

Although Salazar admired Mussolini, he distanced himself from fascism, which he considered a pagan Caesarist political system without legal or moral limits. He said he was opposed to everything that might break up the family, and against irreligion or 'a materialistic conception of life', among other things. Other — if more secondary — leaders of the Estado Novo may have had more radical ideas than Salazar himself. The ideas of the 'National Revolution', of a new type of 'Nation-State', and of a corporatist constitution were also defined by the right-wing political thinker Martinho Nobre de Melo. In an essay entitled 'Beyond the Revolution', which looked ahead at the tasks of the future in the context of the past, Melo spoke of conserving the 'species' through the institution of the family and maintaining 'a stable and natural order through professional corporations'. Conservatism, nationalism, corporatism, but also cultural isolationism were apparently the key notions. Indeed, Melo stressed the need to 'preserve from deleterious influences', the language, the religion, and the 'social morality and patriotic myths' created by 'the race'. A Mussolini-type of aggressive chauvinism should give the nation hope, courage, and energy. The political leadership had 'to feed the national spirit through the cult of traditions and glories of the past, through the daring hope of national aggrandisement in the future — in short, through the concept of an heroic Nation-State'. This kind of exalted nationalist-revolutionary phraseology was very similar to a fascist world view. Perhaps the influence of right-wing radicals, and the fact that a significant part of the political elite was still anti-clerical, caused Salazar to keep Church and State apart and to prevent the Church from becoming a political factor. He argued that the role of the Church should be social, not political, and that a special Catholic political party was unnecessary (only the National Union was allowed). This is also why some of the earlier republican legislation was not fundamentally altered. Religious teaching in schools remained, strictly speaking, voluntary, civil marriages and divorce were retained, and religious oaths not re-established.[99]

In April 1934 Salazar gave a speech on the 'New Era', which he said was now awakening the 'national conscience' and the prestige of Portugal. 'To reach our goal we have experienced a far-reaching revolution in economics, politics, ideas, customs, institutions, and in our collective life.' The National Union was turned into a hierarchically organised party closely intertwined with the state bureaucracy. A Security Police with full powers and a network of informers which included the Church was now in operation.[100] The Estado Novo adopted the same principle of the paramountcy of the State over individual interests as did the Italian and German fascist regimes and, indeed, the Soviet communist regime. In October 1938, when the Salazar regime had already been consolidated, the Slovak autonomists of the Slovak People's Party took power in what had been the eastern part of the Czechoslovak Republic. In March 1939 Slovakia became an independent state protected by Nazi Germany, and evolved into an authoritarian state with an ideology that could be described as half-Catholic, half-fascist—perhaps not much unlike Salazar's Portugal. But the course of events in Slovakia during the preceding two decades had been different in some ways from political developments in Portugal.

Slovakia

The proclamation of the Czechoslovak Republic in Prague on 28 October 1918 was followed by a Slovak declaration of independence from Hungary two days later. This happened in the Slovak town of Martin and, most probably, independent of the Prague proclamation. The Slovaks defined themselves at that historic moment as a branch of the 'Czecho-Slovak nation', an entity whose precise form was yet unclear, but which seemed to imply that the

---

[99] Ibid., pp. 67-8, quoting Melo; see also Meneses, *Salazar*, pp. 76, 162; Kay, *Salazar and Modern Portugal*, pp. 53-5, 63, 68, 359-60; Wiarda, *Corporatism and Development*, pp. 88, 97-8.

[100] Figueiredo, *Portugal*, p. 68 for quotation of Salazar; Birmingham, *A Concise History of Portugal*, pp. 164-5, 169 for a characterisation of his regime.

Slovaks were a separate cultural-linguistic nation that wanted to live in a common state or, perhaps, political nation with the Czechs. The expectation that the common nation was to have a state-political, not a unitary-ethnic character, was expressed by the fact that most Slovaks used the hyphen when speaking of the 'Czecho-Slovak' state or nation, indicating their desire to have a degree of administrative autonomy in addition to retaining their separate language and ethnicity. The Czechs, however, were influenced by the French model of state centralism and were nervous about the autonomist demands of the German and Magyar minorities as well as — potentially — those of the Slovaks and the Ruthenians. By officially absorbing the Slovaks in the leading state-nation, the Czech political leaders constituted a fictional 'Czechoslovak nation' that represented a majority of the total population of the new Czechoslovak Republic. Thus, on grounds of expediency as well as ideology, they promoted a centralistic idea of both the Czechoslovak State and the 'Czechoslovak nation' and rejected using the hyphen when referring to the 'Czecho-Slovak' nation or other autonomist expressions. Some of the Slovaks themselves — those who were closest to the leading Czech politicians — omitted the hyphen as well and supported Czechoslovak centralism and the Czechoslovak idea. But it would seem that most Slovaks continued to cling to the idea of a separate Slovak nationality based on their own language, culture, and historical experience and associated with the expectation of being granted regional autonomy at some point in the near future.[101]

---

[101] In this section we will refer to some publications in English, German, and Slovak which are helpful for international and Portuguese-Slovak comparisons regarding our subject. See Stanislav J. Kirschbaum, *A History of Slovakia: The Struggle for Survival* (New York, 1995) for an English-language work which expresses affinity in a nuanced and reasonable way with the Slovak Catholic and autonomist cause; esp. Chapter 8 for the 1918 revolution and the First Czechoslovak Republic (1918-1938). Still a highly readable work in German, critical of the Republic but not unfair, is Jörg K. Hoensch, *Geschichte der Tschechoslowakischen Republik 1918-1965* (Stuttgart, 1966) with numerous observations on Slovak questions, the author being perhaps the foremost German expert on Slovak history. For more relevant publications, Slovak and other, see below.

However, the question of political administration and Slovak autonomy was just one aspect of what became a complex struggle between 'Czechoslovakists' and Slovak nationalists. At least as important as national ideology and the political-administrative structure of the new state was the antagonism between the politically dominant anti-clerical secularists (mostly Czechs) and the conservative Catholics of Czechoslovakia — especially those of Slovakia, a far more conservative and Catholic-traditionalist land than Bohemia or even Moravia (itself more Catholic and conservative than Bohemia). Views on the Czechoslovak State and cultural-religious profile often overlapped. Thus, the most prominent of the centralist Slovaks after October 1918 was Vavro Šrobár, who became the leader of the provisional Czechoslovak administration in Slovakia after having been appointed 'Minister for Slovakia' in December 1918. Šrobár — a former Catholic turned anti-clerical — tried to exclude the Slovak Catholic politicians as much as possible from the emerging Czechoslovak political organs, a policy he continued during the following year. Both the question of political administration in the new Slovakia, and the question of culture, education, and the position of the Catholic Church and the Slovak People's Party in the secularist Czechoslovak Republic, became controversies weakening the Republic. The Slovak People's Party, led by the Catholic priest Andrej Hlinka, developed into the strongest opposition party in Slovakia, agitating against Prague centralism and 'Czechoslovakism' but also against the liberal, secularist, and anti-clerical attitudes of the leading politicians and the 'anti-Catholic' policies of the Czechoslovak government. Although this party had been a relatively democratic political movement at first, its conservative Catholicism gradually began to incorporate anti-democratic and half-fascist features, which ended up as the ideological basis for an authoritarian regime ruling Slovakia after 1938.[102]

---

[102] See for the contested position of Slovakia in the Czechoslovak Republic and for the Slovak People's Party, the following essays by Jörg K. Hoensch: 'Tschechoslowakismus oder Autonomie. Die Auseinandersetzung um die Eingliederung der Slowakei in die Tschechoslowakische Republik', in Hoensch, *Studia Slovaca. Studien zur Geschichte der Slowaken und der Slowakei* (Munich, 2000), pp. 71-106; 'Die Verfassungsstruktur der ČSR und die slowakische Frage', in ibid., pp. 107-

Following the proclamation of the Czechoslovak Republic in October 1918, a series of anti-clerical and anti-Catholic incidents in Bohemia-Moravia and Slovakia triggered a strong Catholic reaction, especially in Slovakia. On 3 November 1918 a historic statue of the Virgin Mary in Prague was destroyed by a mob. Some of the Czechs sent to Slovakia to take up administrative or teaching posts began to attack the religiosity of the Slovak people, seen by free-thinking Czechs as a sign of backwardness or even reactionary mentality. The response of the leaders of Slovak political Catholicism to this and other problems was swift. On 28 November 1918 the Executive Committee of the Catholic Clerical Council in Slovakia met under the leadership of Hlinka, himself a priest with both political and clerical ambitions. Hlinka and the Catholic Council made a number of demands on behalf of the organised Catholic interests in Slovakia that were presented to the Provisional Czechoslovak Government in Prague. In the background there was clearly a sense of apprehension regarding the cultural and religious policy of the predominantly liberal-minded Czech political elite which had taken over in the new Republic. The Slovak demands included Catholic schools, a Slovak ecclesiastical province under a Slovak bishop, and the elimination of civil marriage. On 19 December 1918 the Slovak People's Party was officially re-established (it had been dissolved shortly before the First World War) and tried to prevent being excluded from political power. The men that had been chosen by Prague and by its 'dictator in Slovakia', Vavro Šrobár, to take up positions in the provisional Slovak administration were mostly people belonging to the Lutheran minority (15-20% of the Slovak population). Similarly, in the Revolutionary National Assembly in Prague, Slovak Catholics were strongly underrepresented as well. In January 1919 Karol Kmeťko—who two years later became

---

153; 'Die Slowakische Volkspartei Hlinkas', in ibid., pp. 199-220; 'Die Grundlagen des Programms der Slowakischen Volkspartei vor 1938', in ibid., pp. 155-98. See for the Slovak People's Party also, Juraj Kramer, *Slovenské autonomistické hnutie v rokoch 1918-1929* (Bratislava, 1962); Róbert Letz, Peter Mulík, and Alena Bartlová (eds.), *Slovenská ľudová strana v dejinách 1905-1945* (Martin, 2006); James Ramon Felak, *"At the Price of the Republic": Hlinka's Slovak People's Party, 1929-1938* (Pittsburgh, 1994); Dorothea H. El Mallakh, *The Slovak Autonomy Movement, 1935-1939: A Study in Unrelenting Nationalism* (Boulder/New York, 1979).

Bishop of Nitra, the most prominent ecclesiastical position in Slovakia—insisted on behalf of the Slovak People's Party that instruction in the primary and secondary schools should be in 'a Slovak and Catholic spirit', and that Church property should remain in the hands of the Church even when it was made available for public purposes. In October 1919 Hlinka was imprisoned after an unsuccessful attempt to address the Paris Peace Conference and demand autonomy for Slovakia. He had pointed to the promises contained in the Pittsburgh Agreement of American Czechs and Slovaks concluded on 30 May 1918, to which the Czechoslovak president Masaryk had been a party. When Hlinka was released shortly before the general election in April 1920, he had earned a reputation as a dangerous and irresponsible opposition figure.

In September 1921 Šrobár, then Minister of Education, withdrew an earlier promise of the Czechoslovak government to give back to the Catholic Church in Slovakia three secondary schools which had been placed under state supervision. This sensitive controversy, dragging on for several years, caused the Slovak People's Party to become an almost permanent opposition party. The party participated in a centre-right coalition government during the years 1927-29, but went definitively back in the opposition following an even more spectacular controversy over the claim of its leading member Vojtech Tuka that after ten years Slovakia had the legal right to secede from the Czechoslovak Republic. Also highly provocative proved to be the institution of an official day of commemoration of Jan Hus on 6 July 1925, which led the Vatican to break off relations with Prague. In the second general election of November 1925 the Slovak People's Party became the largest party in Slovakia and she would retain this position of relative predominance for the years to come.[103] This meant that the political and cultural struggle

---

[103] Kirschbaum, *A History of Slovakia*, pp. 161-168; Felak, "*At the Price of the Republic*", pp. 20-29, 34-36; El Mallakh, *The Slovak Autonomy Movement*, esp. pp. 37-8; Hoensch, *Geschichte der Tschechoslowakischen Republik*, p. 50; Ismo Nurmi, *Slovakia – a Playground for Nationalism and National Identity. Manifestations of the National Identity of the Slovaks 1918-1920* (Helsinki, 1999), pp. 108-123 for an analysis of the complex religious question in Slovakia during the period of national revolution; Joseph A. Mikuš, *Slovakia: A Political and Constitutional History* (Bratislava, 1995), pp. 163-70 for the 'Memorandum of the Slovaks to the Peace

of Slovak conservative Catholicism against liberal secularism, Czechoslovak progressivism, and Prague centralism was assured of a solid basis.

What were the social, cultural, and political conditions in Slovakia which might explain the dominant position of conservative political Catholicism and the rise of a form of nationalism that appeared to move closer to authoritarianism or even (semi-)fascism? It was certainly not only the Slovak national question and the shortcomings of Prague centralism that were responsible for this, although it is true that Czech insensitivity to Slovak cultural identity and the Slovak desire for national autonomy played an important part. But there was more to it, especially in terms of societal and political culture and lack of democratic tradition. A weak ethnic-Slovak middle class, an undeveloped political culture, and the identification of Prague with freethinking, cosmopolitanism, freemasonry, and anti-clericalism may have reinforced the tendency for Catholic nationalism in Slovakia to evolve into a form of fascism by the 1930s or even earlier.

In 1923 Tuka, editor of the press organ of the Slovak People's Party, *Slovák*, founded the paramilitary organisation the *Rodobrana*, which acted as bodyguards for the party's speakers but was prohibited later that year. The *rodobranci* were originally an offshoot of the Catholic youth organisation *Orol*, but they and their successors, the Hlinka Guard, became something rather different. Indeed, in the mid-1930s the Catholic Church distanced itself from the youth organisations of the Slovak People's Party when activity in this field was growing again. Tuka himself became the centre of the most radical Party faction, which included young nationalists, university students, and Catholic intellectuals in Bratislava, some of whom were developing ideas that went further than just conservative Catholicism or Slovak autonomism. Tuka was also in contact with extreme right-wing groups in Europe, including Italian fascists and Hungarian irredentist radicals. In 1929 he was imprisoned, but after his release in 1938 he resumed his role as a radical leader. Until the

---

Conference of 1919' (Paris, September 20, 1919), submitted by Hlinka and four other Slovaks.

1930s the Slovak People's Party, although it included pseudo-fascist elements, was led by priests, Hlinka and later Jozef Tiso, who stood for Slovak autonomy within the Czechoslovak Republic. Later, by 1938, the younger generation in the movement emerged from the new paramilitary organisation, the Hlinka Guard, under the leadership of men like Alexander Mach, Ferdinand Durčansky, and Tuka who advocated separatism, an authoritarian state, and anti-Semitism.

This Slovak development can be seen as proof of Ernst Nolte's argument that Catholicism was the 'father of fascism' with, in the case of Slovakia, a potentially fascist Catholic populist movement being turned into real fascism by the 'second generation' after the mid-thirties and especially after 1938. Nolte, however, does not seem to consider either Hlinka or Tiso as fascists. Hlinka's Slovak People's Party can only be listed as a fascist movement after the setting up of the Slovak puppet state in 1939. Even so, the term 'Clerical Fascism' which has been applied to the Tiso regime is controversial since some historians deny the fascist character not only of the Hlinka movement but even of the war-time Slovak State. The Hlinka movement was conservative-Catholic, ultra-nationalist, and clerical-authoritarian, perhaps in a unique Slovak pattern. Its 'fascist' nature arguably remained 'immature', i.e. pseudo-fascist, proto-fascist, or semi-fascist.[104]

Catholicism, nationalism, authoritarianism

Although the issue of the relationship between conservative political Catholicism and fascism remains an important one and fascist influences certainly existed, it seems more helpful to regard Slovak nationalist Catholicism as an ideology that should be analysed as

---

[104] Felak, "At the Price of the Republic", pp. 30-33; El Mallakh, *The Slovak Autonomy Movement*, pp. 51-2, 82, 210-15; Linz, 'Some Notes Towards a Comparative Study of Fascism in Sociological Historical Perspective', pp. 21, 50; Bela Vago, 'Fascism in Eastern Europe', in Laqueur (ed.), *Fascism*, pp. 215-47, here pp. 216, 237-8; Ernst Nolte, *Die Faschistischen Bewegungen* (Berlin, 1966), p. 277; Maroš Hertel, 'Rozpory v HSĽS v 20. rokoch 20. storočia', in Letz, Mulík, and Bartlová (eds.), *Slovenská ľudová strana*, pp. 181-95 for the internal conflicts in the Slovak People's Party.

largely independent of fascism. Like in the case of Portugal, the most prominent ideological and political leaders of conservative Catholicism in Slovakia should be distinguished from the pure fascists even though some of the former's (younger) supporters were half-fascists or sympathisers with fascism. Indeed, beside Hlinka, the second leading figure of the Slovak People's Party was Jozef Tiso, whose age, intellect, and career are more comparable to Salazar and his role in Portugal. Tiso was a student for the priesthood in Vienna and was ordained in 1910, but he soon proved his abilities in the field of politics as well. He had become acquainted with the Christian Social movement in Austria, with some of its political leaders, and of course with its Catholic and conservative ideology. Tiso was one of many Catholic priests in Slovak politics, and he became a leading ideologist and organiser of the Slovak People's Party. He saw the nation as having a special purpose in God's scheme of things, which implied that the Slovak nation was entitled to enjoying an honourable place under the sun, that is, political autonomy or independence. After having held many positions in the Slovak People's Party and following Hlinka's death in 1938, Tiso became the new party leader, but especially after the release of Vojtech Tuka in the same year, he also had to deal with the proponents of the more radical, pro-fascist wing, including Tuka himself. The latter, not a priest but a lawyer of sorts, wanted to continue his anti-Czech struggle where he had left off in the 1920s when he founded the Rodobrana paramilitary organisation (which was partly inspired by Italian fascism and whose original success he greatly exaggerated). But while Tuka's ideology appeared increasingly pagan-extremist and fascist, Tiso stuck in the main to his older Catholic and Slovak nationalist ideas. These included, however, a belief in authoritarianism and the legitimacy and necessity of one-party rule. After the Slovak People's Party came to power and the Slovak State (with Tiso as president) was instituted in 1939, it also brought a degree of discrimination and political exclusion of the Slovak Lutherans, although the evidence on this is somewhat contradictory. The discrimination and isolation of Slovak Jews was more clear-cut. The first anti-Jewish decree, already proclaimed on 30 March 1939, forbade the Jews from involvement in the manufacture of Christian symbols of faith. This painful measure seems typical of the mentality of a Catholic authoritarian regime and Tiso himself, but the extent of Slovak-State co-responsibility for the Holocaust remains a contested issue.[105]

The ideology of the Slovak People's Party was based on conservative Catholicism and a form of nationalism that was increasingly anti-liberal, exclusivist, and authoritarian. The party began to regard itself as the only legitimate representative of the Slovak people and the Slovak nation. Its principal slogan, 'For God and Nation', expressed its cultural and ideological orientation quite well. Jozef Tiso, the party's principal and arguably most typical and influential ideologist in the 1930s, explained in some articles in *Slovák* in December 1930 that their first and foremost principle was the 'sovereignty of the Slovak nation'. This meant that the concept of nation was of a higher order than the concept of state. Every nation had its own 'moral personality' and historic purpose, which in the case of the Slovaks was attaining political autonomy. Tiso's political and historical philosophy makes us feel that Herderian Romanticism, Catholic thought, and cultural nationalism could well go together. In a lecture given in Prague in 1930 and translated in English as 'The Ideology of the Slovak Populist Party', Tiso described autonomy for Slovakia as the realisation of a thousand-year quest for national self-determination. He placed the Slovak People's Party in the tradition of the Slovak national movement of the nineteenth century, which had demanded recognition of the Slovak nation and political autonomy. Of course he tried to ignore the possible differences between the increasingly plural movement of the nineteenth century and the exclusive claims of the present Slovak People's Party.

Tiso's party regarded itself as the only genuine representative of the Slovak nation. For a time — as *Slovák* suggested on 1 January 1933 — it allowed the small Lutheran Slovak National Party to share the distinction of being true representatives of the Slovaks. But at a

---

[105] Kirschbaum, *A History of Slovakia*, pp. 187-8, 192, 197, 203; Jörg K. Hoensch, 'Die Slowakische Republik 1939-1945', in Hoensch, *Studia Slovaca*, pp. 221-47 for the Slovak State, including its Jewish policy.

lecture in Prague in April 1934, Tiso clearly said that 'the Slovak People's Party is the organised political will of the Slovak nation.' The other major parties were said to be controlled by non-Slovak elements — either by the Czechs or by the Russian communists. The propaganda of the Slovak People's Party placed great emphasis on the idea of national unity, blaming Czechoslovak parties (the Social Democrats, the Agrarian Party etc.) with trying to divide the Slovaks. Another means of trying to get a solid Slovak national bloc behind them was stressing the all-class nature of the Slovak People's Party. While the Czechoslovak parties were said to represent particular social classes (workers, farmers, and so on), the Slovak People's Party claimed to represent all social classes in Slovakia. A group like the Jews, however, was not seen as a group whose support should be sought as well. Those Jews who supported Slovak culture or maintained good relations with party members — and there were some of them — were described with some sympathy. But all other Jews, the great majority of them, were condemned for their Hungarian orientation, their anti-Slovak economic behaviour, or their alleged sympathy for Bolshevism. When in September 1933 the leader of a Jewish organisation in Nitra signed a petition criticising some recent actions of the Slovak People's Party in the area, *Slovák* published some rather extreme articles against the Jews, including 'Jews against the Slovaks' and 'Jews in Slovakia in the Past and Present — They Were Always against the Slovak People, Off Whom They Live.' Such anti-Semitic attacks increased during the 1930s, but the radical party members who controlled the party's press were more hostile to Jews than the moderates. [106]

At the same time, the programme of the Slovak People's Party included political-administrative, social-economic, and cultural-religious demands. The party wanted to move towards Slovak autonomy, increase the employment opportunities for Slovaks, and fight

---

[106] Felak, "*At the Price of the Republic*", pp. 42-45. See Milan S. Ďurica, *Jozef Tiso – slovenský kňaz a štátnik. I: 1887-1939* (Martin, 1992), pp. 153-202 for Tiso's thought on man, family, nation, state, the social question, and the relationship between the Slovak nation and the Czechoslovak State; also for a more pointed summary of Tiso's views, Hoensch, 'Die Grundlagen des Programms der Slowakischen Volkspartei vor 1938', pp. 178-86.

for 'Slovak' and Catholic education. In these endeavours it was frequently frustrated by press censorship and a constant degree of government persecution, including periodic arrests of party members whose public speaking was deemed a threat to the public order or state security. Hlinka himself and especially Tuka were major examples of party leaders who were imprisoned for several months or even years. Most sensitive of all were cultural and religious issues. The Slovak People's Party was intensely aware of the crucial role of education in the development of national and cultural consciousness. Its cultural programme laid its main stress on building up a Slovak national education system and actively opposing 'Czechoslovak' ideas (both in a secularist and a national sense) and anti-Catholic ideology.

When, during the First Czechoslovak Republic, the education system in Slovakia underwent a spectacular expansion on all levels, this great progress was accompanied by the arrival of a large number of often anti-clerical Czech teachers and a 'Czechoslovak spirit' in many of the schools—trends that were resented by the Catholic Slovak People's Party. To counter the idea of a common Czechoslovak nation, Czechoslovak language (really a mystification), Czechoslovak history, or secular Czechoslovak identity, the party proposed in a proclamation issued in December 1932 the establishment of a Slovak School Council with a view to bringing education into the service of Slovak nationalism. Its ultimate aim, indeed, was the Slovakisation of the education system, including the university in Bratislava. The Slovak People's Party wanted all university teaching and administration to be carried on in the Slovak language, which was a rather drastic demand given the presence of large numbers of Czechs at Bratislava's Comenius University. Indeed, the party was particularly concerned about the philosophical faculty and its Czechoslovak spirit, and demanded the creation of a number of new departments in the faculty, including Slovak language, Slovak literature, and Slovak ethnography. The department of 'Czechoslovak language and literature' was to be abolished and non-Slovak professors should hold their posts only until a suitable Slovak replacement could be found. At the high school ('gymnasium') level, the party demanded education in a 'Slovak national spirit', along with Slovak textbooks and, as far as possible, Slovak teachers.[107]

The question of religion was closely connected with education and the Catholic cultural ideals of the Slovak People's Party. The party advocated the creation of a state-funded parochial school system in Slovakia, which it regarded as 'the basis for the moral development of the nation'. This was quite a demand on the state, which apparently was seen as a necessary pillar for facilitating the religious and cultural ideology of the Slovak nationalists and the Slovak Catholic Church. Of course, the Czechoslovak State would refuse to play this role, and even the Slovak State, after March 1939, preferred to keep control over culture and education instead of leaving this to the Church.

Nevertheless, Slovak nationalist morality was dressed in the language of Christian and Catholic ethics, however simplistic or tautological. The electoral programme of the Slovak People's Party of October 1929 stated that 'the Slovak way of life is built on Christian ethics, hence there can be no Slovak way of life without Christian ethics, nor are Christian ethics conceivable without the Slovak way of life.' It is easy to understand that the party insisted that the government return to the Catholic Church the three gymnasia that it had seized after 1918. This was obviously the bare minimum Slovak Catholics wished to retain in a situation where secularisation and anti-clericalism had begun to dominate culture, education, and society. But the party also demanded the establishment of a faculty of Catholic theology at the university in Bratislava, as well as an increase in state salaries for Catholic clergymen. Another party demand was the implementation by the Czechoslovak government of the agreement with the Vatican to restore mutual relations after the 'Hussite' crisis of 1925. Although signed in 1927, its implementation had to wait until the early 1930s. The Slovak People's Party was especially apprehensive about the anti-clerical Slovak Social Democrat Ivan Dérer, who in his capacity of minister of education between 1929 and 1934 planned to unleash a Kulturkampf against Catholic education, an endeavour from which other politicians

---

[107] Felak, "At the Price of the Republic", pp. 47-8.

tried to keep him back. At the same time the Slovak Catholics and nationalists tried to turn a defensive position into an offensive one, and to get more financial support for Slovak cultural institutions. The Slovak People's Party called for increased state support for the Catholic St. Vojtech Society and the Matica slovenská, and for Slovak art and literature. It also demanded the Slovakisation of the Slovak National Theatre, whose predominantly Czech repertoire apparently upset Slovaks from some of the pro-government parties as well as supporters of the Slovak People's Party.[108]

Differences in outlook and tradition between Slovaks and Czechs were also expressed in other ways. The Slovak People's Party often complained about the thoroughness with which the Czechoslovak tax collectors did their job in Slovakia. But it is also true that the party wanted to protect those Slovaks who did not have much tax money to pay . Influenced by the papal encyclical *Quadragesimo anno* (1931), the party advocated a 'just wage' for workers and employees in Slovakia, that is, enough earnings to cover their material and cultural needs. Employment for the working class and state jobs for the Slovak intelligentsia, but also state contracts for Slovak businessmen and better prices for peasants, all figured in the party's programme.

In this regard, it is also interesting that the Slovak People's Party had its own ideas in the field of foreign policy. It opposed foreign minister Edvard Beneš's policy of relying on the Western powers, especially France. Long before the fatal Munich Agreement of 1938, the party already warned against such one-sided overreliance. It argued for better relations between the Czechoslovak Republic and authoritarian right-wing states like Poland, Italy, and Austria. Karol Sidor and some other party leaders, citing a common Slavic origin and Catholic faith, called for close relations between Czechoslovakia and Poland. In 1933 Štefan Onderčo, the party's spokesman on foreign policy, proposed the inclusion of Poland in the Little Entente. On the other hand, the treaty of mutual assistance that Czechoslovakia signed with the Soviet Union in 1935 (partly

---

[108] Ibid., pp. 48-9.

on the urging of France) was bitterly denounced by the Slovak People's Party.

Thus, the Slovak Catholic nationalists developed their own vision on what was the national interest of Slovakia, which was based on their cultural and national ideology and on their strategy of trying to gain short-term advantages whenever circumstances permitted. This actually helped them to prepare for taking power after October 1938. Gaining autonomy or independence for Slovakia and establishing their exclusive power in an authoritarian state had become one and the same thing for the Slovak People's Party. Although Slovakia was forced by circumstances and by Nazi-Germany to proclaim state independence in March 1939, there is little evidence that the leaders and supporters of the party were concerned with trying to preserve parliamentary democracy or even the last remnants of the liberal political order. Of course there were sincere democrats in the Slovak People's Party too, but the ideology and political mentality of a growing number of its members were not compatible with liberal democracy.[109]

Conclusions

The victory of the 'political Counter-Reformation' in Slovakia in 1938-39, which lasted for only six years in contrast to its protracted Portuguese counterpart, was the result of a combination of factors, some of which had a more general European significance and some of which were, perhaps, unique to the Slovak situation or to Central Europe. Of course, the exceptional conditions on the eve of the Second World War were another crucial factor in the case of Slovakia. This historical factor at the end of the period covered by this essay was less important in the case of Portugal. But in other ways the respective situations in both countries are historically comparable, with both similarities and differences being significant in the context of European, regional, and national political Catholicism.

The political dynamics of Catholic Slovak nationalism were fed by a tradition of cultural conservatism which existed in many

---

[109] Ibid., pp. 50-54, 215.

parts of Europe, including Portugal, Spain, Austria, Poland, and other countries. It was also shaped by the historic Slovak national question, a problem that was typical of the political landscape of East-Central Europe and which was inherited by the First Czechoslovak Republic. The Slovak People's Party was the expression of both of these cultural-political dimensions, that is, the conservative-Catholic and the Slovak-national one. This, of course, is what made it possible for the party to become a major player in the new democratic Slovakia and the Czechoslovak Republic after 1918. The results of the Czechoslovak general elections of 1925 and 1935 show that about half of all ethnic Slovaks — not to be confused with all voters in Slovakia, one third of whom belonged to non-Slovak minorities — tended to support the national and cultural programme of the Slovak People's Party.[110] However, the other half did not, and this had a lot to do with the relative success of the Czechoslovak Republic, a stable and democratic state — indeed increasingly exceptional in Central Europe in the inter-war years — which offered new opportunities to its citizens both politically, culturally, and to some extent, economically. The Slovak people, including the supporters of conservative political Catholicism, benefitted a great deal from the modern conditions of the Republic, particularly in terms of the new democratic culture and modernised system of education. But it was precisely these aspects which also enabled the Slovak People's Party to voice its grievances against those features of the new Republic which it found repulsive: the domination of politics, society, and public culture by the progressivist, anti-clerical political forces and the hegemony of the Czechs and their Slovak 'Czechoslovakist' supporters, almost all of whom were opponents of political Catholicism and the radical autonomist programme of the Slovak People's Party. In contrast to Portugal, the institutions of the Czechoslovak State were loyal to the republic. Therefore, it took the Central European crisis of the late 1930s, from the viewpoint of Czechoslovakia largely an external one, to provide the Slovak

---

[110] The Slovak social democratic leader Michal Korman had the courage to declare in 1947, during the legal proceedings against Tiso, that after 1935 at least 50 percent of the Slovak population were in favour of autonomy; see Hoensch, 'Die Grundlagen des Programms der Slowakischen Volkspartei vor 1938', p. 176.

autonomists with the historic opportunity to break away from Prague, seize power in Slovakia, and establish an authoritarian regime which has been defined by many historians as 'clerical fascism'. Quite aside from the merits of this disputed label, this did not mean that there were no legitimate grievances in Slovakia or, indeed, mass support for the Slovak People's Party's take-over. The truth is that there was.

The situation in Portugal was rather different in several ways. The Portuguese Republic founded in 1910 was the result of a progressive coup d'état by lower-rank army officers supported by various groups of republican and liberal politicians and anti-clericalists. The level of support for this republican revolution was probably lower than was the level of support among ethnic Slovaks for the Czechoslovak revolution in 1918. Despite the original enthusiasm for the Portuguese Republic in its first months or years, it soon became clear that a substantial proportion of the Portuguese population, especially outside the capital Lisbon, were sceptical about the republican regime, its unfulfilled promises, and its rather extreme anti-clerical course. In Portugal, of course, there was no national issue to mobilise support either for the revolution itself or for its opponents, although both sides claimed to speak on behalf of the true interest of the nation. The republican anti-clerical measures provoked a strong backlash on the part of the conservative section of the Portuguese nation, including prominent Catholic intellectuals and several right-wing groups, and therefore proved divisive to the point of triggering civil war or counter-revolution. The republican politicians themselves were divided as well, and it is an unfortunate fact that the Portuguese First Republic was chaotic and politically unstable almost from the start.

Although in Slovakia the Czechoslovak anti-clerical policies were divisive too, even the supporters of conservative Catholicism tended at first to welcome the Czechoslovak revolution because it meant the national liberation of the Slovak people from the old Hungarian regime. This attitude began to change over the course of the years, and the grievances of Slovak conservative Catholics, which had already been expressed at an early stage, now were compounded by their national-autonomist strivings, which helped to increase the number of supporters of the Slovak People's Party. However, Czechoslovakia as a whole remained under the domination of the Czechs and even the anti-Czechoslovakist Slovaks hesitated for a long time to squarely oppose the existing Republic. In Portugal, on the other hand, the Republic was contested and rather unstable from the start, while some institutions in the country began to sabotage her either openly or in secret.

It was, again, the Portuguese army — if this time the middle and higher ranks — which played a leading part in looking for an alternative to the existing political order, now represented by the increasingly dysfunctional liberal republic. The Catholic Church, some of the (non-liberal and non-urban) dominant classes, and conservative intellectuals like Salazar played their part as well. Salazar and other right-wing, Catholic, and authoritarian thinkers were able to construct an ideological alternative to the failing liberal perspective and divided democratic republicanism of their adversaries. The thought and traditions of the Catholic Church played a significant role in all of this, especially from a cultural and ideological point of view. However, in Portugal there was no successful mass-political party led by Catholic priests as there was in Slovakia. Instead of a conservative Catholic party similar to the Slovak People's Party led by a charismatic leader like Hlinka, Salazar used other political techniques to gain power between 1926 and 1932. The groups and individuals he got behind him included conservative army officers, state bureaucrats, and anti-liberal or even anti-democratic political figures. For Salazar, the Church had a social, cultural, and ideological function, not primarily a political one. The same held true for one or other Catholic political party, which he preferred to replace with a national party on a broader and more authoritarian political basis.

After seizing power in 1938-39, the Slovak People's Party became in fact a kind of national or state party as well, but in Slovakia there was a closer historical link between Church and party based on the older Central European tradition of political Catholicism, in which priests played a leading role in terms of party organisation and political ideology. This social, political, and cultural tradition of political Catholicism could assume the character of modern

Christian Democracy or that of a more anti-liberal and anti-modern right-wing movement. In Slovakia the anti-liberal and right-wing tendency was reinforced by the dynamics of the national question during the First Czechoslovak Republic, although fascist or pseudo-fascist influences played a part as well. Fascist influences, both foreign and Portuguese, were important in Portugal too, but both in Portugal and Slovakia there was a difference between the real fascists on one side and the authoritarian 'political Counter-Reformers' on the other side.

The worldview of these protagonists and ideologists of the political Counter-Reformation, and the political conditions of the first half of the twentieth century that may explain it, constitute the principal topics of this essay. As far as the authors of this article are aware, an explicit comparison of Portugal and Slovakia in terms of this problem has never been attempted before, although pieces of relevant historical material are mentioned by analysts of comparative fascism. We want to repeat that conservative or anti-liberal Catholic movements are not necessarily the same thing as fascist movements. To argue otherwise would be tantamount to historical simplification. However, it is also true that the two types of movement overlapped to some extent, particularly as far as ideas on social order (corporatism, enforced social peace), hierarchy (authoritarianism, political inequality), and anti-liberalism (rejection of individualism or even of multi-party democracy) are concerned.

Of course, there were variants of Catholic authoritarianism in different countries at different historical moments, and the degree to which it resembled forms of fascism varied as well. The core ideas of Catholic political philosophy could be interpreted in various ways by different individual thinkers and in different historical and political situations. There was a basic difference between those Catholic movements which developed into modern Christian Democracy, and those which could not resist the old temptation of hierarchical thinking and anti-liberalism. In countries where democratic traditions were weak but the Catholic tradition strong, the anti-democratic alternative could become a serious option. Both Portugal and Slovakia were examples of this, and the fact that at one point the anti-clerical enemies of political and cultural Catholicism began to assert themselves meant that the conservative

Catholic political forces had to organise a new Counter-Reformation movement. This new political movement could be a political party, as in Slovakia, or a coalition of traditionalist and anti-liberal groups, as in Portugal. This type of Catholic movement proved able to influence the course of modern European history. The question is whether similar (religious) or competing (neo-fascist) types of anti-liberal alternative have new chances in our own time.

7. Authoritarianism in crisis: Portugal, Czechoslovakia, and '1968'

This article presents a comparative analysis of political developments in Portugal and Czechoslovakia during the 1960s and early 1970s, focusing on the historic year '1968' and its preconditions. The two countries experienced authoritarian regimes that went through a crisis of both a systemic and a moral kind, reaching a climax in 1968. In Czechoslovakia the liberalisation policy of Alexander Dubček and his reform-communist coalition triggered spontaneous political and cultural activities among the population, which became a threat to the system of one-party rule. The Warsaw Pact invasion in August 1968 put an end to this experiment and the illusion of reform communism. The analysis of the causes, contradictions, and failure of liberalisation remains a challenging subject for contemporary historians. Comparing the Czechoslovak experience with the evolution of the right-wing dictatorship in Portugal during the same period, may help to deepen our understanding of the nature and limits of authoritarianism in Europe. In Portugal the persistent regime of António Salazar came to an end in the same year 1968 after a series of political crises in the 1960s had shown its weaknesses and the inevitability of reform. However, his successor Marcelo Caetano maintained the regime's authoritarian core and only carried out some cosmetic changes to keep Portugal with its colonies afloat. The Portuguese had to wait until 1974 for the regime to collapse, a short period of time, however, compared with the twenty-one more years that the Czechs and Slovaks had to wait. The extent of political space for opposition activity and the nature of elite disunity are among the critical questions examined in this article, which makes a comparison of Portugal and Czechoslovakia a challenging endeavour.

The concept of 'authoritarianism' is probably the most appropriate one when looking for a term to include, define, and compare both 'left-wing' and 'right-wing' dictatorships in Europe in the second half of the twentieth century. The extent to which political, social, or cultural space was granted to the citizens of authoritarian regimes varied from case to case, with 'totalitarianism' at one extreme and relatively mild dictatorships at the other extreme. When authoritarian regimes entered a temporary or definitive phase of crisis, civil disaffection among their citizens might erupt into a newly created public space and pave the way for successful opposition movements. In 1968, and perhaps already at some earlier moments in the 1960s, such nascent movements were suppressed in both Czechoslovakia and Portugal. However, the fact that civil disaffection, political criticism, and signs of regime crisis had emerged at all, showed that the authoritarian regimes were unlikely to survive forever. It depended on the economic, social, and international conditions, authoritarian-elite stability or disunity, and the strengths and weaknesses of potential opposition figures or smaller groups whether or not authoritarianism would be able to extend its life much further. The communist regime in Czechoslovakia eventually lasted for a good forty-one years, the right-wing dictatorship in Portugal (1926-1974) even longer.

With the help of analytical concepts such as 'authoritarianism', 'regime crisis', 'political space', and 'civil disaffection' we will address the following research questions: How and why did crisis phenomena begin to undermine the authoritarian regimes of Portugal and Czechoslovakia? Who were the principal subjects, groups, or institutions that began to voice criticism of particular features of the regimes? Which political-elite divisions and changing authoritarian strategies may be discerned, and how did developments play out over the course of the 1960s? How and why did the two regimes survive the crisis of 1968? Against this backdrop, the most significant political developments in Portugal will be discussed in the next section, followed by an analysis of the developments in Czechoslovakia. Thereafter, some conclusions and additional comparative observations will be made that may be helpful in trying to improve our understanding of the changing character, the strengths and weaknesses, and the mutual differences and similarities of the two authoritarian regimes.

Portugal:
the last phase of right-wing authoritarianism

António de Oliveira Salazar was an authoritarian political leader, economist, and Catholic intellectual who shaped to a significant extent the modern history of Portugal between the 1920s and 1960s. He is taken seriously by historians and is an example of the great importance of the individual in the history of Europe. He helped to suppress Portuguese liberal democracy after the military coup d'état of 1926, and acted as prime minister from 1932 to 1968, an incredibly long period. He gradually increased his power during the 1930s when his regime became semi-fascist and openly anti-democratic, although Salazar himself always remained in the background.[111] After World War II, the Portuguese dictatorship had to show a more moderate face and to suggest that it tolerated at least a limited degree of criticism or political opposition. When Salazar became incapable of ruling the country in September 1968, the reins of the regime he had created were taken over by the technocratic and pragmatic Marcelo Caetano until the 'Carnation Revolution' of April 1974, which started the process of democratic transition.

Salazar's long period of authoritarian rule was almost unique in Europe and only matched by the Spanish dictator Francisco Franco (1939-1975); Stalin ruled only for about 25 years. Salazar's dictatorship was based on the ideology of a rather harsh and racist Portuguese nationalism, the conservative principles of traditional Catholicism, and a non-parliamentary form of pseudo-democracy and functional economic and social representation known as 'corporatism'.[112] He also created a political party, the National Union, the only party tolerated in Portugal. Only members of the National Union could sit in the National Assembly, but this quasi-

---

[111] The Czech historian Jan Klíma describes him as 'the silent dictator'; see his *Salazar, Tichý diktátor* (Prague, 2005). See for other useful works on Salazar and his authoritarian regime Hugh Kay, *Salazar and Modern Portugal* (New York, 1970); Antonio de Figueiredo, *Portugal: Fifty Years of Dictatorship* (Harmondsworth, 1975); Filipe Ribeiro De Meneses, *Salazar: A Political Biography* (New York, 2009).

[112] See Howard J. Wiarda, *Corporatism and Development: The Portuguese Experience* (Amherst, MA, 1977).

parliamentary body had no real power. In Salazar's 'New State' (*Estado Novo*) the security police PIDE played an important role, and freedom of the press or other forms of political expression or oppositional activity were scarcely permitted. Only in the 1960s did a greater measure of political expression begin to surface among some groups of Portuguese citizens, including protests against the authoritarian state itself and against Portugal's disastrous colonial wars in Angola, Mozambique, and Guinea-Bissau.

Although in the 1950s and 1960s Portugal went through the early stages of economic modernisation, the nation was not able to eliminate the old problem of rural poverty and mass emigration. The regime tried to reduce the level of emigration by introducing restrictive administrative measures, but this only caused a rise in illegal emigration. After World War II the pace of emigration, including illegal emigration, was increasing continuously. Between 1946 and 1973 two million people left Portugal, almost half of them between 1966 and 1973, when annual numbers were rising sharply. Most of the nearly one million Portuguese who left the country during the period of 1966-1973 went to France and other West-European countries to work as unskilled labourers. By 1967 their remittances to their families had overtaken the Portuguese colonial economies as sources of foreign exchange. Despite these benefits, the regime in general and Salazar in particular experienced the mass emigration and selling of human capital on such a large scale as a defeat and a loss of face.[113] Yet, Salazar did not seem very concerned about the backwardness of Portugal or the poverty of the people, seeing them instead as a guarantee of stability. In Portugal in 1960 per capita annual income was just $160, compared with $219 in Turkey. Infant mortality was the highest in Europe and 32 percent of the population was illiterate.[114]

Between 1947 and 1962 there were three abortive military coup attempts, initiated by low-paid and reform-minded junior army officers who were angry about the stagnation of the country.

---

[113] Meneses, *Salazar*, p. 563-564; David Birmingham, *A Concise History of Portugal* (2nd ed., Cambridge, 2003), pp. 176-178.
[114] Tony Judt, Postwar: *A History of Europe Since 1945* (London, 2005), p. 511.

Other events which damaged the image of Salazar were the opposition to his regime by a prominent Portuguese army general, Humberto Delgado, in the late 1950s and early 1960s, and perhaps even more so the criticism of the Bishop of Oporto. Delgado was eventually murdered under mysterious circumstances in 1965, while the Bishop of Oporto, who had addressed Salazar in a long letter in July 1958 to demand more social and political freedom, was silenced in a more subtle way by exiling him to Italy.[115] Salazar could not understand why the Catholic Church in Portugal, which had been protected by him since he came to power, should want to express any criticism to his rule or tolerate 'progressive' elements within its ranks. But how much and what kind of opposition was there among the mass of Portuguese people against the authoritarian state? J.W. Lennon, the Irish ambassador in Lisbon, wrote in March 1961 that in his opinion, 'the average Portuguese while not entirely satisfied with the regime is prepared to tolerate it. Many remember the pre-Salazar chaos of 1910-1926 and all have been indoctrinated with the view that a change would mean a return to the conditions then prevailing.'[116] His successor as Irish ambassador, Count O'Kelly de Gallagh, an admirer of the regime, was not so sure however. In 1962 he experienced the May Day demonstrations in Lisbon, which the Portuguese Communist Party (PCP) had attempted to turn into a show of force. This caused some unease with him personally, and also in wider conservative and official political circles. However, the most serious problem, especially in the eyes of Salazar, was the growing rift between his regime and the Catholic Church, in which more progressive and democratic tendencies were emerging both in the Vatican and in Portugal.

Although outsiders often exaggerated the conservative Catholicism of the Portuguese, criticism of political and social conditions by some of the major bishops was a notable and, for many, unexpected phenomenon. The Bishop of Oporto had been a problematical critical voice in recent years, and in the early 1960s the

---

[115] See for the criticism expressed by the Bishop of Oporto and the ensuing conflict between him and the Salazar regime, Meneses, *Salazar*, p. 438-447.
[116] Quoted in ibid., p. 566.

Bishop of Beira, in Mozambique, appeared to become another one. He was a reform-minded man and wanted to see Portugal live up to its 'spiritual mission' in Africa in a more serious, humanitarian, and positive Christian way. In 1964 tension erupted between Salazar and the Pope, Paul VI (1963-1978), himself. Paul VI was critical about the lack of political freedom and democracy in Portugal as well as about Portuguese colonialism and the sour Portuguese attitude to India. Goa, the Portuguese territory in India, had been lost in 1961, and when the Pope wanted to attend the Eucharistic Congress in Bombay in 1964, an infuriated Salazar wrote to him:[117]

> In Rome, perhaps, they ignore the difficulties faced and the greatness of the work carried out by this regime in order to allow the Catholic Church to enjoy the possibility of expansion, since I became, in some measure, responsible for the course of public life. In the Vatican much is thought about Christian Democracy, and about liberalism, and progressivism is permitted. May God not allow me to see the result of such doctrines and attitudes applied in Portugal. Since the advent of liberalism [in Portugal] Catholics have endured a lot, and even more since the founding of the Republic, with its Jacobinism. If the Church desires its return, then it is because it no longer wants saints, preferring instead to have martyrs.

In October 1965 the Portuguese foreign minister, Franco Nogueira, expressed his horror at the Pope's praise for the United Nations in New York, where Paul VI had gone to deliver a speech. The Pope described the United Nations as 'the ideal of which humanity has dreamt through its pilgrimage across time', and as part of 'God's design'. Representatives of African countries were delighted and regarded the Pope's critical reference to colonialism as an attack on Portugal.[118] Two months earlier, in August 1965, a remarkable Catholic pamphlet had circulated in Portugal, being posted also to parish priests in rural areas and claiming to be the voice of a 'Christian Movement for Democratic Action'. Its author was Joaquim Pires de Lima, a progressive priest. The pamphlet stated:[119]

> The Portuguese situation is anti-Christian. The national economy's structures rest on a plutocracy and on the formation of capital at the expense of a

---

[117] Quoted in ibid., p. 571.
[118] See ibid., p. 573.
[119] Quoted in ibid., p. 574.

> low standard of life for the working classes... There is no longer emigration but rather a mass exodus. The Portuguese have no present and do not believe in the future... We demand the right to dialogue. The presence of Catholic thought in Portuguese life is justified by eight centuries of history.

Such conclusions were reached by Catholic intellectuals who were in tune with events in the outside world and who were increasingly influential in the Catholic Action movement. This old-established movement had a tradition of cultural conservatism, but also of social reform-mindedness. The use of terms like 'Catholic thought' and 'dialogue' expressed a desire for social and political reforms and a more open and democratic debate. Younger Catholic intellectuals wanted a 'dialogue' even with Marxists and social reforms of a more radical nature.[120] The new Catholic intellectuals were acting independently, but their ideological guidance was coming from abroad, not least from the Vatican itself, which had entered a more progressive phase in its history during the pontificate of Paul VI's predecessor Pope John XXIII (1958-1963).

In April 1963 John's encyclical *Pacem in terries* affirmed that the laws which govern men had been inscribed by God 'in man's nature'. This meant that, to share in God's authority and partake of the resulting legitimacy, governments must respect the rights of men. The encyclical expressed a democratic principle: 'The fact that authority comes from God does not mean that men have no power to choose those who are to rule the State or to decide upon the type of government they want...' Men had, as a bare minimum, a right to be informed of the affairs of their state. In March 1967 Pope Paul VI issued another encyclical, *Populorum progressio*, which went even further in that it criticised colonial attitudes and policies. It declared that it was 'quite natural for nations with a long-standing cultural tradition to be proud of their traditional heritage. But this commendable attitude should be further ennobled by love, a love for the whole family of man. Haughty pride in one's own nation disunites nations and poses obstacles to their true welfare.'[121]

---

[120] H.V. Livermore, *A new history of Portugal* (2nd ed., Cambridge, 1976), p. 356.
[121] Quoted in Meneses, *Salazar*, p. 574. The premature death in 1963 of John XXIII, the Pope who had initiated the reforms of the second Vatican Council, was

Portuguese Catholics found it hard to square this sentiment with their government's explanation of the colonial wars in Africa. Such disaffection as there was in Portugal at this time was reinforced by the domestic problem of poverty. This was probably the greatest source of discontent with the regime not only among lower-class but also among middle-class people, more so even than the lack of democracy or the terrible colonial wars. However, the latter two problems became more critical in the late 1960s.

In 1967 Paul VI visited Portugal to mark the fiftieth anniversary of the Fátima apparitions, a major event for the country. At first Cardinal-Patriarch Manuel Cerejeira, the highest ecclesiastical office-bearer in Portugal, was pessimistic about the Pope accepting the invitation from the Portuguese Church, given his bad relationship with Salazar. Salazar hoped to exploit the Pope's visit as proof of the Vatican's support for the Portuguese regime. The Pope and Salazar met only briefly on 23 May 1967, on the margins of the event which drew as many as 1.5 million people to Fátima. The gulf between the two men was too wide to be bridged, and in Portugal itself Church-State relations were to suffer another blow the following year. In Lisbon a well-known priest, José da Felicidade Alves, had begun to express his concern about the Portuguese colonial wars to his parishioners. After theological studies in Paris, Friar Alves became even more outspoken, and around Easter 1968 he distributed a document which criticised the war, the actions of the security police PIDE, and censorship. It also called for a social and political revolution in Portugal. The radicalised priest returned to Paris for further studies, but his text began to circulate in Portugal, and by January 1969 there were already seven editions. In reaction, Alves was dismissed by Cardinal Cerejeira.[122] The hierarchy of the Portuguese Church tried to keep the situation under control and to avoid conflict with Salazar. But in addition to the Church, there were also other circles in Portuguese society where opposition and unrest were brewing.

---

greeted with relief by the Portuguese church hierarchy; see Birmingham, *A Concise History of Portugal*, p. 181.

[122] Ibid., p. 575.

In the early 1960s Portuguese university campuses became an ideological battleground in which the government seemed to be in retreat. In 1962 there were riotous student actions which the regime desperately tried to suppress, and on May Day of that year there were strikes, demonstrations, and violent confrontations on the streets of Lisbon comprising both workers and students. Many were arrested and imprisoned, including some 1,200 students. According to the British newspaper *The Observer* of 21 May 1962, the regime was facing the most serious threat for years in the shape of two separate attacks: student unrest and worker actions.

Students desired above all academic freedom and wanted the police to be kept out of the university. Marcelo Caetano, who became Salazar's successor as prime minister in September 1968, was at this time Rector of the University of Lisbon and actually resigned his position because of the presence of the police on university grounds. Traditionally, the police did not enter the precincts of the university, but this unwritten rule had been breached. Caetano wrote an article in the monarchist-Catholic newspaper *A Voz*, criticising the restrictions imposed on the autonomy of universities by new laws introduced by the government. He even resigned from the executive board of the National Union, the official ruling party. Even if this was not the result of fundamental political differences with Salazar but more a question of mutual irritations within the power elite, it was an expression of elite disunity. The academic authorities were jealous of their status, prestige, and independence and felt humiliated by the presence of police officers at the university. They ignored Salazar's plea to accept the government's repressive university policy. The rift deepened when 300 arrests were made at the conservative University of Coimbra. The protesting university students were from different political backgrounds: their numbers included Leftists, Catholics, and even some from the radical Right. Wider political issues were not explicitly articulated, but rather the independence of the university, which was seen as an island where free speech should be allowed. But even this was politically significant, because it challenged and contradicted the principles of the authoritarian state and might ignite protests among other sections of the population.

Indeed, the defence of the privileged status of university student was not accepted by the regime, which felt it could not risk making any such concessions, especially in a situation in which it was engaged in an escalating war in the African colonies. But the repression was imperfect. The oppositional radical newspaper *República* continued to appear in Lisbon despite difficulties with the censorship. Those on the Left who were not allowed to enter the teaching profession or the university often qualified as lawyers, swelling the considerable number of oppositional figures in the legal profession, especially in Lisbon. Examples were the lawyers Álvaro Cunhal, a leader of the Communist Party, and Mário Soares, a radical socialist.[123]

Restoring order to the universities was one thing, dealing with an old enemy like the Portuguese Communist Party (PCP) another. Cunhal had escaped from Peniche prison in 1960 and in the following year was reconfirmed as secretary-general of the party. Cunhal's escape revitalised the PCP but also led to the destruction of its more liberal wing. Under Cunhal's leadership, the party stood out for its loyalty to Moscow and, after the late 1960s, its rejection of 'Euro-communism' supported by the more reform-minded Italian, Spanish, and most other West European communist parties. Indeed, this orthodox attitude did not change after the suppression of the Prague Spring in 1968, although some Portuguese communists who had experienced Dubček's liberalisation policy and the subsequent Warsaw Pact invasion in their Czechoslovak exile, disagreed or even left the party.[124] Mário Soares, who later became the leader of the Portuguese socialists, had left the PCP by 1965 and founded

---

[123] Figueiredo, *Portugal*, p. 221; Meneses, *Salazar*, p. 576; Livermore, *A new history of Portugal*, pp. 356-357.

[124] Pavel Szobi, 'From Enemies to Allies? Portugal's Carnation Revolution and Czechoslovakia, 1968-1989', *Contemporary European History*, Vol. 26, No. 4 (2017), pp. 674-676. See for the PCP also Alex Macleod, 'Portrait of a Model Ally: The Portuguese Communist Party and the International Communist Movement, 1968-1983', *Studies in Comparative Communism*, Vol. 17, No. 1 (1984); for the contrast with the Euro-communist Spanish party and its tense relationship with the Soviet Union, Maud Bracke, *Which Socialism, Whose Détente? West European Communism and the Czechoslovak Crisis of 1968* (Budapest, 2007).

with some others a new left-wing party, Portuguese Socialist Action.

Since the PIDE managed to contain the communists and other political opposition groups reasonably well, Salazar and his government were probably more worried about the students' revolt in France in May 1968. The Portuguese dictator, who admired de Gaulle greatly and had come to rely on France's international support during his presidency, was shocked by the speed with which the internal political crisis in France occurred and by de Gaulle's inability to contain it. On 9 June 1968 Salazar said to his foreign minister, Franco Nogueira, that de Gaulle was 'following a difficult path—that of concessions. He will no longer be de Gaulle. We must admit that his decline has begun.'[125] Salazar was resolved to meet any such outbreak of dangerous opposition with force. In this effort he demonstrated both his anxiety and his pettiness. In early June 1968 he expelled a Belgian dance choreographer, Maurice Béjart, from Portugal after his troupe had put on a ballet performance in Lisbon. The performance took place just after the murder of Robert Kennedy, and in the final scene the dancers shouted 'make love not war', while one of the voices was denouncing war and other injustices. At a council of ministers a few days later, an exasperated Salazar declared that 'here things must be different. There can be no crisis of authority: when the first symptom manifests itself, we must solve the case radically, whatever the cost, be it with students or workers.'[126] He urged better sharing of information among government services and Portuguese institutions with international contacts in order to keep out foreigners with dangerous views and to avoid embarrassing situations.

Although Salazar was in many ways intolerant and narrow-minded, he also had less repulsive features, especially his austerity and incorruptibility. This became even more notable as his political efficiency declined during the course of the 1960s, because it showed the contrast between himself and his entourage. Salazar's

---

[125] Memoirs of Franco Nogueira, *Um político confessa-se* (Oporto, 1986), p. 300, quoted in Meneses, *Salazar*, p. 577 n97.
[126] Nogueira, *Um político confessa-se*, p. 301, quoted ibid.

declining grip on details was one reason why there emerged more space for some spontaneous and oppositional political expression, despite the lawless behaviour of the PIDE. Corruption was a growing problem, influencing the Portuguese state and society as Salazar entered his old age and inevitable decline. *The Observer* wrote of him on 21 January 1962 that, 'himself incorruptible, he has sometimes helped to corrupt his subordinates by allowing them to secure rich material rewards — and by making it plain that he despises their greed.' Salazar had hoped to lead by example, but most powerful men around him saw his austere life as just an eccentricity. He never acted to investigate accusations against ministers and others for enriching themselves at the public's expense, preferring instead to let them suffer from rumours about their dismissal, before he finally dismissed them.

Although corruption became even more damaging in the eyes of the public during the war in Africa, nothing was done. In 1963 and 1967 British newspapers reported several serious cases of economic and moral corruption, including the notorious case of an organised prostitution ring involving teenage call-girls, the so-called *ballet rose* sex scandal. On 11 December 1967 the *Daily Telegraph* reported: 'Portugal's 76-year-old dictator is accused in the reports of personally suppressing the prosecution of at least one Minister and other "establishment" figures charged with corruption for fear of the consequences to his regime if the scandal became public knowledge.' Mário Soares, who had tried to exploit the limited political space as an opposition leader in the 1965 National Assembly elections, was accused of providing this information to the foreign press and arrested. He was deported to the island of São Tomé by order of Salazar, where he would stay for nearly a year. When the Minister of Justice, Antunes Varela, wanted to prosecute the ringleaders of the sex scandal, he was forced to resign. The regime and Salazar became the laughing stock of Europe, but a communiqué of the National Union distributed to the movement's cadres in January 1968 declared: 'Against calumny we advance the truth.' It was increasingly difficult for the government to decisively influence public opinion, because the official political organisations and press organs were in a bad state. Salazar and his loyal inner circle became more isolated, and the issue of succession ever more pressing.[127]

During the 1960s there had emerged an increasingly diverse constellation of political figures and interest groups around Salazar, including some talented and ambitious government ministers, different Catholic organisations, monarchists, and others. This made it difficult to predict who might eventually become the successor of the ageing dictator. Of interest in this regard is the rivalry between the conservative Catholic organisation Opus Dei, whose power was on the increase, and the more progressive Jesuits, who were not willing to let this happen. Opus Dei tried to attract Marcelo Caetano, still an influential university professor, into its orbit, but failed in this endeavour on account of his bad relationship with other prominent Portuguese figures who were members of the organisation. The relationship between Opus Dei and the Jesuits was so bad — the PIDE reported that they were 'sworn enemies' — that the Apostolic Nuncio in Lisbon had to intervene to keep the peace.

By the summer of 1968 Salazar seemed to be losing his mind given his irrational outbursts, with the American ambassador in Lisbon, W. Tapley Bennett, wondering in a report to Washington if he was 'senile'.[128] On 6 September 1968 Salazar fell from a deckchair and developed a cerebral stroke. Later that month the titular president of Portugal, Admiral Thomaz, called upon Caetano to become acting prime minister. Salazar, physically and mentally incapable, was not informed; he finally died in July 1970. Like Salazar four decades earlier, Caetano was invited to step into the government as an intellectual saviour who could resolve the tensions within the power elite. In 1959 Caetano had resigned from the government after disagreements with Salazar, returning to academic life in the University of Lisbon. In his youth he had been more right-wing than Salazar, but later he became more pragmatic and embraced what was ironically described by some as 'liberal fascism' or 'forward-looking traditionalism'.[129]

---

[127] Meneses, *Salazar*, pp. 588-590; Figueiredo, *Portugal*, p. 224.
[128] Meneses, *Salazar*, p. 596.
[129] Figueiredo, *Portugal*, p. 220.

When the succession crisis came up in 1968, it proved, against the expectations, not to be a crisis at all, because Caetano was backed by most of the key figures in the regime. His disengagement from the regime during the 1960s actually worked in his favour, with the bulk of the middle class, including the more critical elements, being prepared to accept his leadership. Caetano was sufficiently identified with the regime to provide continuity and seen as sufficiently flexible to allow evolution. He reminded the Portuguese that they were used to the rule of 'a man of genius', but must now accustom themselves to government by lesser men.[130] Caetano, paraphrasing de Gaulle, stated that he was 'neither left nor right – but for the country'.

While a hard-liner like foreign minister Nogueira eventually resigned and several others were dismissed, some government ministers adopted a more liberal posture, speaking of a 'political spring'. In December 1968 the restriction on votes for women was removed, and in the spring of 1969 an effort was made to bring in candidates with liberal views for the National Assembly elections in October. Among the opposition politicians there were communists, socialists, and Catholic progressives, but in the end they were all marginalised in what was a questionable electoral process. Of the more liberal candidates for the National Union only a dozen were elected. Caetano brought some younger members of Catholic Action into his cabinet, and the Bishop of Oporto, who had been prevented from re-entering Portugal after a visit to Rome in 1958, was allowed to return, as was Mário Soares. In a speech to the newly elected National Assembly in November 1969, Caetano reaffirmed his desire for national reconciliation, but the elections had been a sham as in the days of Salazar. In 1971 the group of tolerated liberals in the National Assembly went into opposition against Caetano when he rejected a relaxation of the censorship. His regime did not go further than implementing some cosmetic changes, causing people to cynically observe that if the Portuguese had not achieved a parliamentary democracy they had at least moved on to the stage

---

[130] Livermore, *A new history of Portugal*, p. 358.

of 'Fascism with a human face'.[131] A number of oppositional 'publishing co-operatives' were at first allowed to operate, but in 1972 they were suppressed. During the elections for the National Assembly in 1973 some opposition meetings were allowed and could briefly function as a school of democracy. But they could not change the reality of the authoritarian regime and the opposition protested that a number of their lists had been disallowed.[132]

In light of all this, it is questionable whether Portugal experienced a true liberalisation under Caetano, even if some people dubbed his policies a 'spring' as in Czechoslovakia under Dubček. Pavel Szobi calls Caetano an example of the technocratic second generation of the authoritarian elite, who were willing to let others share power with the state apparatus as long as it would help the country modernise and remain stable.[133] But Salazar was a technocrat of sorts with pragmatic features as well, despite his semi-fascist authoritarianism. He started out as a financial expert and 'technocratic dictator', became more ideologically focused in the 1930s, reverted to a more pragmatic and moderate stance after the war, and all along remained a paternalist and nationalist autocrat, a conservative intellectual, and indeed a technocrat who understood the need for the occasional reform.[134] In other words, Salazar was both a conscious technocrat and a dictator who neglected his people, while his mode of repression has been described as 'controlled repression'.[135] Reform and repression were not necessarily in contradiction, both being selective and focused on a combination of regime continuity and pragmatic adjustment. This held true for Caetano's policies too, and for both men authoritarianism apparently

---

[131] Figueiredo, *Portugal*, p. 225. Was this reaction inspired by the Prague Spring and its suppression?

[132] See for the succession of Caetano and developments until the revolution of April 1974 Meneses, *Salazar*, pp. 590-602; Figueiredo, *Portugal*, pp. 217-28; Livermore, *A new history of Portugal*, p. 357-371.

[133] Szobi, 'From Enemies to Allies?', p. 671. Szobi refers to Caetano's own interpretation of the 'reforms' in his memoirs; Marcelo Caetano, *Depoimento* (Rio de Janeiro, 1977).

[134] See Birmingham, *A Concise History of Portugal*, pp. 132, 164.

[135] Tom Gallagher, 'Controlled repression in Salazar's Portugal', *Journal of Contemporary History*, Vol. 14, No. 3 (1979).

meant keeping control while experimenting with shifts in policy, including expanding and contracting political liberalisation. The contrasts between them were smaller than the similarities were. This was a major difference with the situation in Czechoslovakia, where a liberalising regime was succeeded by a retrogressive neo-authoritarian one.

Czechoslovakia: crisis, reform, and the restoration of communist authoritarianism

How did Czechoslovakia go from a regime crisis and a period of liberalisation and reform policy to a fully fledged neo-authoritarian restoration? The move away from Stalinism came late in Czechoslovakia, because almost all communist leaders were co-responsible for the terror of the early 1950s. As late as 1961 Antonín Novotný, first party secretary since 1953 and president since 1957, dismissed as 'irresponsible' the petitions for a review of the purge trials of 1949-1954. When a review board was finally appointed in August 1962 to inquire into the Slánský and other political show trials, this happened under pressure of Khrushchev. The board sat during 1962-1963 and the purpose behind it was to acknowledge the regime's recent criminal past without loosening control. Several surviving victims had been quietly released in the late 1950s, but without exoneration or rehabilitation. Some were later rehabilitated, often by the same figures who had condemned them ten years earlier, because the old party leadership remained largely intact. Also typical was that the statues of Stalin in Prague and Bratislava were only removed in October 1962, much later than in other East European countries. When in 1963 the rehabilitation of Slánský and other trial victims was officially to be announced, it even had some international implications. The Italian communist leader Palmiro Togliatti secretly wrote to Novotný asking him to delay the news until after the forthcoming Italian elections. Togliatti understood that not only the Czechs and Slovaks but also many Italians would be disgusted at their communist leaders' earlier collaboration in covering up judicial murder.

What made the situation in Czechoslovakia special was also the fact that the consequences of the communist revolution had been felt more intensely there than in other Eastern European countries. Czechoslovakia was not only economically more developed than most of the other nations (or indeed than Portugal) but in many ways a middle-class society with a well-educated population. The victims of the Stalinist terror in Czechoslovakia had often been intellectuals, many of them Jews. Those social classes which did not belong to the 'working class' as defined by the communists had suffered downward social mobility. The percentage of working-class children in higher education rose from under 10 percent in 1938 to 40 percent in 1963, but the level of higher education declined. According to the new centralistic Constitution of 1960, Czechoslovakia had advanced to 'full socialism' with class antagonisms overcome, but by the early 1960s the country suffered from economic stagnation and even regression. The party congress in December 1962 therefore decided to start decentralising reforms in order to revive the economy and correct the poor planning. By 1965 some local initiative was permitted, and factories were allowed to purchase their own raw materials and could even retain their profits for sharing among their workers or for re-investment. However, proposals by Ota Šik and other reform economists such as using factory profits as incentives for the workers were not popular with party hardliners, and were only endorsed in 1966.[136]

The combination of public rehabilitations, acknowledgement of Stalin's faults, and the prospect of further reforms opened the way to a more serious questioning of the party's stranglehold on society and public life. Although the economic reforms were not

---

[136] Galia Golan, *The Czechoslovak Reform Movement: Communism in Crisis, 1962-1968* (Cambridge, 1971), pp. 4-8; Joseph Rothschild and Nancy M. Wingfield, *Return to Diversity: A Political History of East Central Europe Since World War II* (3rd ed., Oxford/New York, 2000), pp. 166-167; Roderick Phillips, *Society, State, and Nation in Twentieth-Century Europe* (Upper Saddle River, N.J., 1996), p. 413; Tony Judt, *Postwar: A History of Europe Since 1945* (London, 2005), pp. 436-437. Works like those by Judt, Phillips, and Rothschild and Wingfield look at Czechoslovak developments from a comparative and European perspective, which is helpful in understanding them. For Portugal such comparative observations are more difficult to find in the literature.

always popular among the workers, they certainly were among writers, teachers, artists, and intellectuals who were hoping for a loosening of the party regime, enabling them to produce critical publications and engage in new activities. In 1963 a writers' conference in Liblice was devoted to Franz Kafka, thus breaking a taboo in communist Czechoslovakia. Kafka had anticipated in some of his works the nightmare of bureaucratic rule, and discussing them was one factor leading to a liberalisation of public debate.

This debate also included the fate of those murdered by Stalinism; political myths such as the story of massive anti-Nazi resistance during World War II; and forbidden subjects like the *nomenklatura*'s lust for power and the growing disillusionment with communism. At the Slovak Writers' Congress in April 1963, Ladislav Novomeský, a rehabilitated Slovak writer, admiringly referred to his 'comrade and friend' Vladimír Clementis, one of the victims of the Slánský trial.[137] After the fall of Khrushchev in 1964, the increasingly liberal climate in Czechoslovakia continued, allowing space for critical essays, novels, films, and stage-plays. At the Fourth Czechoslovak Writers' Congress in 1967, Milan Kundera, Ludvík Vaculík, Pavel Kohout, and Václav Havel attacked the communist leadership for the 'material and moral devastation' it had wrought. They called for a return to the cultural heritage of Czechoslovakia and for the country to take up again its 'normal' place in a free Europe. This was language with a radicalising potential, and a challenge to the one-party state. Student unrest in Prague in October 1967 over the rigid structure of party youth organisations and bad housing conditions met with a violent police reaction. The old Novotný leadership wanted to clamp down on the intellectual opposition, but were probably held back by two considerations. One was the need to pursue at least some of the economic reforms, which implied a degree of dissenting opinion (since in neighbouring Hungary such liberalising policies had proved successful). The

---

[137] Elena Londáková, 'Ladislav Novomeský v slovenskom kultúrnom kontexte po roku 1945', in Miroslav Pekník and Eleonóra Petrovičová (eds.), *Laco Novomeský. Kultúrny politik, politik v kultúre* (Bratislava, 2006), pp. 62-63.

other consideration were the emerging difficulties in Slovakia, where the call for greater autonomy became louder.

The Slovaks had benefited more from communist economic policy than the Czechs, since urbanisation, industrialisation, and even agrarian collectivisation had brought material improvements to the poor Slovak population. However, by the early 1960s the stagnation of the economy hit the new heavy industry of central Slovakia harder than any other industry, and Slovak workers in the less skilled industrial branches felt adversely affected by some of the economic reforms. In the political field the Slovaks resented the insufficient rehabilitation of the victims of the purges, because some Slovaks had not been included. Furthermore, the Constitution of 1960 reduced even further such limited autonomy as had previously existed in Slovakia.

When the economic regression became apparent in 1962, the Slovak communists, who had long been subjected to centralising pressures and humiliation by their disdainful Czech comrades, decided to exploit the problems of their greatest tormentor, Novotný. In their campaign to disgrace Novotný they employed the help of critical writers and philosophers, who were given access to Slovak party publications in which they articulated a mixture of Slovak-national, humanistic, and Marxist grievances. In response, Novotný tried to activate the latent anti-intellectualism of the workers — with some success, but insufficient to stop his critics. In April 1963 Novotný could not prevent that his critic Alexander Dubček became first secretary of the Slovak Communist Party, although he was present at the meeting where this decision was made. After this defeat he stormed out of the meeting and never again attended a plenum of the Slovak Central Committee. Later that month came the Slovak communists' rehabilitation of the Slovak victims of the 1949-1954 purges, deliberately done in advance of Prague's decision on the recommendations of the review board. In May 1964 the Slovaks attained the formal restoration of some of the Slovak autonomous institutions that had been abolished by Novotný's 'Socialist' Constitution of 1960, although not yet in terms of their real powers. By the end of 1966 the Slovak party had removed from its Presidium and Secretariat all the centralistic figures whom the Prague party leaders had imposed on it over the previous two decades. In 1967, Dubček, the leader of the Slovak party, criticised the low share of investment being directed towards Slovakia, an example of inequality between the Czech lands and Slovakia. Another increasingly influential and critical Slovak communist was Gustáv Husák, who had been in prison for nine years on the accusation of 'bourgeois nationalism'. After his release in 1960 he began to build a following amongst students in Bratislava, increasing his popularity through his articles in *Kultúrny život*, the Slovak writers' weekly.[138]

Another significant example of the growing criticism of prevailing conditions in Czechoslovakia was the pressure by the legal profession to restore the rule of law in its original sense, which meant independence of courts and judges, protection of the rights of citizens and defendants, and no presumptions of guilt by probability, class background, or other unlawful considerations. Between 1963 and 1966 some laws and decrees were adopted which were officially meant to correct the 'distortions of socialist legality' rampant since 1948.

The effectiveness of these juridical rectifications depended on further political and societal reforms. In 1967 Novotný should have started to implement the more drastic economic and administrative reforms recommended by the party experts. Their proposals for further decentralisation and increased local autonomy were welcomed in Bratislava, even though a reform such as profit-related wage incentives did not appeal to the unskilled workers in Slovakia's inefficient industrial plants. But Novotný had been overwhelmed by doubts and now resisted any loosening of central

---

[138] Judt, *Postwar*, pp. 437-439; Rothschild and Wingfield, *Return to Diversity*, pp. 167-168; Kieran Williams, *The Prague Spring and its aftermath: Czechoslovak politics, 1968-1970* (Cambridge, 1997), p. 48; Phillips, *Society, State, and Nation*, p. 413; Miroslav Londák, Stanislav Sikora and Elena Londáková, *Predjarie. Politický, ekonomický a kultúrny vývoj na Slovensku v rokoch 1960-1967* (Bratislava, 2002) for Slovak developments; for the rise of Husák in the 1960s Michal Štefanský, 'Pokusy Gustáva Husáka o návrat do politiky', in Slavomír Michálek and Miroslav Londák (eds.), *Gustáv Husák. Moc politiky, politik moci* (Bratislava, 2013), pp. 513-526; Milan Zemko, 'Od straníckeho reformátora k normalizátorovi. K publicistike Gustáva Husáka v rokoch 1963-1968', in ibid., pp. 527-542; Viliam Plevza, *Vzostupy a pády. Gustáv Husák prehovoril* (Bratislava, 1991), pp. 45, 62-79.

party control. He tried to exploit the anxieties of the industrial workers, many of whom felt threatened by the consequences of the reforms such as wage differentiation, quality-work expectations, and plant closings in inefficient sectors. In the end, his attempted sabotage of the reform proposals further alienated both reform-minded communists and Slovak autonomist communists. Slovak communists began to talk of the need for federalisation of the state, and of the difficulties of collaborating with the *apparatchiks* in Prague. Echoing old complaints of social groups such as Slovak building workers and Slovak teachers, they felt slighted by the dominant Czechs and pointed to the purges of so-called 'bourgeois-nationalist' Slovak communists in the 1950s and even to pre-war indignities. The national problem was a critical factor in Czechoslovakia, and one reason why Novotný could not do what Gomułka and his minister of the interior Moczar had done in Poland — dividing the workers and intellectuals by using anti-Semitic demagogy.[139]

The winter of 1967-1968 was the crucial moment when the reform policy would either have to be pressed more vigorously, or be rolled back. In late December 1967 Novotný contemplated a military coup, but the army's Political Directorate suppressed it. On 5 January 1968 the Central Committee ousted Novotný from the party leadership (from the presidency only on 22 March) and elected Dubček first secretary. As leader of the Slovak Party for the past five years, he appeared to many to be both a credible and a reassuring candidate. He was a veteran though relatively young *apparatchik* who believed in the system but supported reforms; who was a friend of the liberal intellectuals; and who, as a Slovak patriot, might appease Slovak resentments. In February 1968 Dubček and the party leadership gave their approval to the stalled economic reform programme, which also included the agrarian sector.

---

[139] See for the situation in Poland in 1967-1968, Judt, *Postwar*, pp. 433-436; Rothschild and Wingfield, *Return to Diversity*, pp. 191-195; Philip Longworth, *The Making of Eastern Europe. From Prehistory to Postcommunism* (2nd ed., London, 1997), p. 55, where the observation is made that in contrast to Czechoslovakia, students and intellectual dissidents in Poland in 1967-1968 were isolated from the people and party reformers. This had been different in 1956, however, and would also be different in the 1970s.

Dubček's more relaxed attitude appealed to the young, and his declaration of loyalty to the party, socialism, and the Warsaw Pact initially reassured the Soviet leadership as well.[140]

Dubček wanted political reforms to renovate Czechoslovakia's socialist system, and economic reforms to revitalise its economy. He wanted to gain public confidence by making the reforms a reality for the people, which implied making governmental and social institutions more independent of the party. At the same time, he wanted to maintain the dominant position and control by the party, preventing liberalisation from spilling over the limits set by Soviet hegemony. Since these objectives were complex and contradictory, it is unclear to what extent Dubček really knew where he wanted to go.[141] He allowed a vast public debate with unpredictable long-term consequences. A stream of dismissals and resignations, and even several suicides, ensued in the ranks of Novotný's old guard as one institution after another were taken over by the reformers. Dubček and his reformist allies became engulfed by a spontaneous liberalisation movement, which initially remained within the channels of official policy but by the middle of 1968 began to get out of control.

At first Dubček's ambiguity—'socialism' vs. democratisation—worked in his favour, as various political factions, interest groups, and cultural associations, which had sprouted up on all sides, offered him their support. Within a short span of time, an active public opinion developed and with it a sense of mass participation in all kinds of public activities—in other words, an expanding social, political, and cultural space of freely acting citizens, the

---

[140] Judt, *Postwar*, pp. 439-440; Rothschild and Wingfield, *Return to Diversity*, pp. 168-169; Phillips, *Society, State, and Nation*, p. 413.

[141] For different views of Slovak historians on these questions, see for example Ivan Laluha, 'K charakteru reformného hnutia v 60. rokoch. Osobnosť Alexandra Dubčeka', in Ivan Laluha, Eleonóra Petrovičová and Miroslav Pekník (eds.), *Alexander Dubček. Politik, štátnik, humanista* (Bratislava, 2009), pp. 100-113; Stanislav Sikora, 'Politické pôsobenie Alexandra Dubčeka v rokoch 1963-1968', in ibid., pp. 114-131; Stanislav Sikora, 'O jednom významnom dokumente', in ibid., pp. 132-147. For the effort to liberalise public administration and its reversal after 1968, Jozef Žatkuliak, 'Úsilie o liberalizáciu verejnej správy 1967-1968. Politická "pacifikácia" národných výborov 1969-1970', in ibid., pp. 162-179.

hallmark of a civic society. Public opinion surveys were organised, making it possible to establish the views of Czechoslovak citizens.[142] Public rallies in Prague in the weeks following Dubček's election demanded greater press freedom and a genuine inquiry into the Stalinist purges and the responsibility of the old Novotný guard. Carried on this wave of popular enthusiasm and expectations, Dubček allowed a relaxation of censorship, which was tacitly ended in early March and formally abolished in June. He initiated a purge of Novotný supporters from the party and the army, with Novotný himself being replaced as president by General Ludvík Svoboda. The Slovaks actually wanted Husák or Novomeský as new president, and the Czechs had other candidates too. In April Husák became a deputy prime minister with responsibility for constitutional reform, including the federalisation of Czechoslovakia.[143] This was not unimportant with a view to his later role as a 'normaliser', who, as a popular Slovak, also had the potential to pacify Slovakia.

In early April the Central Committee finally adopted an 'Action Programme', which had long been prepared and discussed. It called for a reduced role for the state on the path to socialism, more freedom for industry and agriculture, 'democratisation' of the economic and political system, a relationship of equality between Czechoslovakia and the Soviet Union, the withdrawal of all Soviet military advisers, an equal status and autonomy for Slovakia within Czechoslovakia, and a rehabilitation of all past victims of the purges. It anticipated a wide range of civil liberties (but not

---

[142] Jaroslaw Piekalkiewicz, *Public Opinion Polling in Czechoslovakia, 1968-1969: Results and Analysis of Surveys Conducted during the Dubcek Era* (New York, 1972).

[143] Williams, *The Prague Spring and its aftermath*, pp. 74-75; Karel Kaplan, *Mocní a bezmocní* (Toronto, 1989), p. 95; Stanislav Sikora, 'Politický vývoj na Slovensku v rokoch 1968-1971', in Miroslav Londák, Stanislav Sikora and Elena Londáková, *Od predjaria k normalizácii. Slovensko v Československu na rozhraní 60. a 70. rokov 20. storočia* (Bratislava, 2016), pp. 35-44 for Slovakia; Elena Londáková, 'Kultúra v zovretí politiky', in ibid., pp. 260-295 for Slovak cultural developments in 1968; Jozef Žatkuliak, 'Činnosť tzv. Husákovej vládnej komisie a proces prípravy federalizácie Československa', in Michálek and Londák (eds.), *Gustáv Husák*, pp. 559-582; Michal Macháček, *Gustáv Husák* (Prague, 2017), pp. 378-387, who calls Husák the 'spiritual and real father of the federation.'

freedom of association or for other political parties), a strengthening of parliament and the courts, and, interestingly, recognition of the State of Israel. The Programme envisaged that the Communist Party should maintain its leading role while being more sensitive to the needs of specific interest groups, and spoke of 'a unique experiment in democratic communism'. Only after a transition period of ten years, the party would allow the formation of other political parties and the holding of multi-party elections.

The publication of the Action Programme may have encouraged the idea that the new reforms and freedoms could be integrated into the 'socialist' project. The enthusiasm among the population for 'socialism with a human face' was genuine and it may be wrong to suppose that the people wanted to re-introduce 'capitalism'. The idea that a 'third way' was possible — a democratic socialism compatible with representative institutions and individual freedoms — had captured the imagination of Czechoslovak intellectuals, reform communists, and the wider population. This was understandable against the background of the relatively broad support that the Communist Party had enjoyed in Czechoslovakia. In December 1967, party members constituted 16.9 percent of the Czechoslovak population, a higher proportion than in any other communist state. It was widely believed that the distinction between the old Stalinism and the renewed socialist idealism of 1968 was based on real possibilities.[144] In his preface to a third report on the Czechoslovak political trials, commissioned in 1968 by Dubček but suppressed after his fall, Jiří Pelikán asserted that 'the Communist Party had won tremendous popularity and prestige, the people had spontaneously declared themselves for socialism.'[145] Even if this was an exaggeration, the state of public opinion nourished both idealism and illusions.

---

[144] Judt, *Postwar*, pp. 440-441; Rothschild and Wingfield, *Return to Diversity*, pp. 169-170; Phillips, *Society, State, and Nation*, p. 414.

[145] Jiří Pelikán (ed.), *The Czechoslovak Political Trials. The Suppressed Report of the Dubček Government's Commission of Inquiry, 1968* (Stanford, 1971), p. 17; see Jiří Pelikán, *Socialist Opposition in Eastern Europe: The Czechoslovak Example* (New York, 1976) for another example of optimism about a 'socialist' alternative to authoritarian communism.

While many people may have believed that socialism could be saved from the Stalinist past and that the party could make this happen, the reform communists themselves hoped that they could manage this without losing control. A new government headed by Prime Minister Oldřich Černík was installed on 18 April as, presumably, a meaningful parallel institution alongside the party. Parliament had become more involved in governing too, and even rejected some of the legislation submitted to it. Changes to the electoral law made in 1967 had already allowed the possibility of rival candidates. Encouraged by public demonstrations of support, including in the traditional May Day celebrations, the government relaxed virtually all formal controls on public expressions of opinion. On 26 June two official announcements were made: censorship of press and media was formally abolished, and Czechoslovakia was to become a federal state comprising a Czech and a Slovak Socialist republic.

In the summer months of 1968 the country experienced a ferment of reform activities and initiatives, some of it going further than what the party envisaged. Indeed, some of the moderate reformers began to talk of a 'rightist threat' and 'counter-revolutionary' activities. Unions of farmers (a quarter-million strong), veterans, and artisans were formed. Councils were set up in factories to look after workers' interests during the transition to the new, more decentralised and democratised economy. The government made some concessions on political associations, although it refused to allow the re-establishment of the Social Democratic Party, which had been absorbed by the Communist Party in 1948. Concessions were made to the churches as well, allowing them to offer religious education and re-establish youth organisations. The churches were among a host of marginalised social and cultural institutions in communist Czechoslovakia, especially the Catholic Church, the largest denomination in the country and traditionally strong in Slovakia. During the liberalisation process young people showed a growing interest in religion which even the clergy found amazing. In June 1968 a Catholic seminarian in Bratislava told the author and researcher Paul Neuburg: 'We knew some of them believed, but their campaigning for the freedom of worship, the numbers that come to mass, the letters of support they write to the Catholic paper, have all been surprises to us.'[146] Even so, religious freedom and freedom of expression were short-lived phenomena in Czechoslovakia and largely disappeared after August 1968. The federalisation of the state was the only reform that survived, becoming law on 28 October 1968.

In June the dynamics generated by liberalisation led to increasingly radical demands and expectations, which was logical but also fraught with danger. Why wait ten years for free and open elections? And why retain state control and ownership of the media now that censorship had been abolished? On 27 June *Literární listy* and other publications carried a manifesto issued by the writer Ludvík Vaculík, 'Two Thousand Words', addressed to 'workers, farmers, officials, artists, scholars, scientists and technicians'. It called for the re-establishment of political parties, the formation of citizens' committees to defend and advance the cause of reform, and other steps towards further change beyond the party's control. The people needed to press the communist reformers to move forward, but also had to act themselves. Vaculík warned that the battle was not yet won, because the reactionaries in the party would fight to preserve their privileges, and there also was talk of 'foreign forces intervening in our development' (Moscow had already expressed its reservations in April). This was too much for Dubček, who disavowed the manifesto as provocative and rejected Vaculík's idea that the communists should abandon their monopoly of power. A shift towards 'bourgeois pluralism' was not acceptable to the convinced communist Dubček, in whose eyes the party was the only appropriate vehicle for change if the vital elements of a socialist system were to be preserved. He believed that the party was supported by the people, even if they did not immediately act upon Vaculík's increasingly popular manifesto. The party's credibility might increasingly rest upon its willingness to pursue changes which would ultimately drive it from its monopoly of power: an unsolvable dilemma. As Tony Judt observes: 'The fault line

---

[146] Paul Neuburg, *The Hero's Children: The post-war generation in Eastern Europe* (London, 1972), p. 109.

between a Communist state and an open society was now fully exposed.'[147]

The radicalisation went on, even within the party leadership. By August 1968 the reform process seemed to have become unstoppable, while not only the conservative but also the moderate party wing around Dubček himself began to have their doubts about the outcome. New laws were promulgated which introduced an unprecedented level of democracy into the party and the political system. Party and state offices were to be separated; a limit was placed on the number of terms an office-holder could serve; and secret ballots were introduced. The leading role of the party was re-affirmed once again, but its hesitant and contradictory policies had begun to diminish its influence. The scale and speed of the changes had produced alarm among conservative communists, who saw their system sliding away. Communist leaders in Moscow and Eastern Europe were anxious about the effects of the reforms on their own citizens, some of whom travelled to Czechoslovakia to become infected with the new ideas while others escaped to the West using Czechoslovakia's lax travel policies.

Dubček's belief that he could keep Moscow at bay was probably his greatest illusion. He tried to convince the Soviet leaders that they had nothing to fear from the events in Czechoslovakia, but in fact everything to gain from the popularity of the reformist Czechoslovak Communist Party and the faith in a rejuvenated socialist project. The Czechoslovak reformers believed that the Hungarian mistake of 1956 had solely been Hungary's departure from the Warsaw Pact. They had perhaps not fully grasped that the Hungarian crisis was related to the loss of the Communist Party's monopoly of power. The Polish leader Gomułka was angered by public criticism in Prague at Poland's wave of almost official anti-Semitism, and various Eastern bloc leaders had other complaints. Dubček insisted that free speech did not undermine control by the party or their resolve to keep their obligations to the Warsaw Pact. However, the

---

[147] Judt, *Postwar*, pp. 441-442 (p. 442 for the quotation); Williams, *The Prague Spring and its aftermath*, Chapter 4; Rothschild and Wingfield, *Return to Diversity*, pp. 170-171; Phillips, *Society, State, and Nation*, pp. 413-414.

fact that the uncensored Czechoslovak press was publishing the work of Soviet dissidents and that Russian students visiting Prague could hear opinions that were banned at home was seen by Moscow as a very serious issue.

By July, following the appearance of the 'Two Thousand Words' manifesto, Moscow had come to the conclusion that the Czechoslovak events were spinning out of control. On 3 July Brezhnev warned: 'we cannot remain indifferent to the fate of Socialism in another country.' On 11 July *Pravda* compared the situation in Czechoslovakia to that in Hungary in 1956, although there was no violent turmoil in Czechoslovakia at all. At a meeting in Warsaw on 14 July, Eastern European leaders, with the exception of the Czechoslovaks, were warned in an official letter of the risk of counter-revolution. The document stated that 'the situation in Czechoslovakia jeopardises the common vital interests of other socialist countries', and demanded that the country re-impose censorship, curb its intellectuals, and reverse its liberalising reforms. Dubček refused to comply, and when he and Brezhnev met two weeks later he tried to convince Brezhnev again that the Czechoslovak party was not jeopardising its position but strengthening its public support. Dubček was told by his reformist colleagues not to waver and that 'the nation and the party will sit in judgment'. At a Warsaw Pact meeting in Bratislava on 3 August Brezhnev presented the doctrine that would be named after him: 'Each communist party is free to apply the principles of Marxism-Leninism and socialism in its own country, but it is not free to deviate from these principles if it is to remain a communist party... The weakening of any of the links in the world system of socialism directly affects all the socialist countries, and they cannot look indifferently upon this.'[148]

Yet one week later a draft was published in Prague of new party statutes, to be confirmed at an Extraordinary Party Congress on 9 September. They required the election of party officials by secret ballot and permitted minorities to maintain and defend their political views, a move away from Leninist 'democratic

---

[148] Judt, *Postwar*, pp. 442-443; Rothschild and Wingfield, *Return to Diversity*, pp. 171-173; Phillips, *Society, State, and Nation*, p. 414.

centralism'.¹⁴⁹ This possibly played a part in the Soviet decision to intervene in Czechoslovakia, even if such a step was already being prepared. Open critique of the Soviet Union in Czechoslovak publications had become part of the problem as well, which must have made Dubček realise that he was losing control. In a telephone conversation with Brezhnev on 13 August, Dubček explained that he was trying to suppress popular criticisms of the Soviet Union, but 'this issue cannot just be solved by a directive from above.'

He did not know that on 3 August five of his colleagues on the party's Presidium had secretly handed the Russians a letter describing an imminent threat to the socialist system and requesting military intervention. At a secret meeting in Hungary two weeks earlier, Vasil Biľak, one of Dubček's opponents, had been told by the Ukrainian party leader Petro Shelest that Moscow would like to have a 'letter of invitation'. The ensuing letter, hardly a spontaneous one, referred explicitly to the party's 'loss of control', the 'risks to socialism', and the likelihood of a 'counter-revolutionary coup'. It requested 'intervention and all-round assistance', but also that their statement be treated 'with the utmost secrecy'. The Kremlin apparently expected that a sharp intervention could prompt the conservatives in the Czechoslovak Central Committee, almost half of its members, to rise up against the liberalisation and the new party statutes. This, they hoped, would draw the workers away from the intelligentsia and, through promises of federalisation, the more nationalistic Slovaks from Dubček's reformers.

The Soviet decision to invade was not formally taken until 18 August, but intervention was probably seen to be inevitable by July at the latest. The Soviet leaders feared that the Czechoslovak Party Congress on 9 September might see a further acceleration of reformist and democratic policy, and were truly frightened of its impact upon other communist states. When 500,000 Warsaw Pact (overwhelmingly Soviet) troops marched into Czechoslovakia on 21 August 1968, they met with massive non-violent resistance — partly organised by workers who had hitherto been wary of the

---

[149] Robin A. Remington (ed.), *Winter in Prague: Documents on Czechoslovak Communism in Crisis* (Cambridge, MA, 1969), Document 43.

reform movement. All in all, street protests and a few more violent acts of resistance resulted in some 200 fatal casualties. The unfriendly reception surprised the Soviet leadership, who had been led to expect by, presumably, a combination of wishful thinking and unreliable information that their tanks would encounter widespread support. Dubček and some of the other Czechoslovak leaders were arrested, flown to Moscow, threatened, and obliged to sign a paper renouncing parts of their programme and agreeing to the Soviet occupation. But when shortly afterwards the Kremlin was forced to accept that the reformers had the support of the Czech and Slovak people, it decided to conclude an 'agreement' with them. Dubček remained in office for the time being, a censorship law was passed, and the Czechoslovak government allowed Soviet troops to be stationed temporarily in the country.[150]

However, the repression of the reform programme began immediately and became euphemistically known as 'normalisation', although it was nothing less than an interrupted revolution.[151] The party congress was cancelled, censorship was re-introduced, and the Action Programme was mentioned no more. Brezhnev chose to let Dubček stay in office a few months longer to see how events unfolded. He also decided to push the federalisation of Czechoslovakia with the aim of splitting the Slovaks — whose chief demand of autonomy was to be conceded — from the Czechs, who were more focused on defending democratic reforms than on federal reconstruction. In the industrial towns of Bohemia and Moravia there briefly emerged a network of workers' councils on the model of those in Hungary in 1956.[152] At their peak in January 1969 they claimed to represent one sixth of the national workforce, but they were weak in Slovakia. That month also saw the suicide of Jan

---

[150] Judt, *Postwar*, pp. 443-444; Rothschild and Wingfield, *Return to Diversity*, pp. 171-173; Phillips, *Society, State, and Nation*, pp. 414-415.
[151] H. Gordon Skilling, *Czechoslovakia's Interrupted Revolution* (Princeton, 1976).
[152] Vladimír Fišera (ed.), *Workers' Councils in Czechoslovakia, 1968-1969. Documents and Essays* (London, 1978). The evidence on the role of the working class is contradictory: wariness of the reform movement existed alongside an opposition movement of workers' councils. Of course, there were different localities and different groups of workers, and attitudes may have shifted over time.

Palach, whose funeral on 25 January became an occasion for national mourning.

In April 1969 demonstrators took to the streets following Czechoslovakia's victory over the Soviet Union in a crucial ice hockey game. The Kremlin exploited the occasion to remove Dubček and replace him with Gustáv Husák, who as a Slovak and former victim of Stalinism was the ideal figure to carry out the job of 'normalisation.' The ensuing repression was less brutal than in the past, but effective. There were no public trials or executions but in the course of the next two years the Czechoslovak Communist Party was purged of all its 'unreliable' elements, with 90 percent of those expelled being Czechs. People who had been active or prominent during the liberalisation period were 'interviewed' and asked to sign statements renouncing their actions and rejecting the reforms. Most signed; those who refused lost their jobs and, along with their relatives and children, became social pariahs. The largest group of victims were those who had played a visible cultural or intellectual role, including journalists, writers, and student leaders. The Czechoslovak Security Police even seems to have established a special unit to monitor the country's Jews, possibly triggered in part by the fact that František Kriegel, the only one in the group of leaders brought to Moscow in August 1968 who refused to sign the document renouncing their actions, was also the only Jew.[153]

The post-reformist message of the normalisation regime was that in 1968 the country had passed through what was depicted as a psychosis of abnormality, with false prophets exploiting the hysteria.[154] Now the nation had to be directed back to the correct path, which was to be achieved by the carrot of reasonable material conditions and the stick of omnipresent surveillance. The people were being humiliated and made complicit in their own defeat, which

---

[153] Judt, *Postwar*, p. 445 n15.
[154] This 'psychological language' is interesting. In January 1970, in a speech on 'consolidation', Husák spoke of ensuring 'a quiet life for people' and the advantages of predictability as opposed to the uncertainty of the reform period; see Williams, *The Prague Spring and its aftermath*, pp. 40-41. See for Husák's statements in the early years of normalisation Norbert Kmeť, 'Politický vývin Československa v 70. rokoch 20. storočia (prejavy a state G. Husáka)', in Michálek and Londák (eds.), *Gustáv Husák*, pp. 610-636.

helped to break resistance. By 1972 the 'restoration of order' had become a reality,[155] with playwrights forced to do cleaning jobs, university lecturers stacking bricks, troublesome students expelled, the police files full of useful 'confessions', reform communists cowed, and 80,000 Czechs and Slovaks in exile.[156]

There were some protests against the occupation of Czechoslovakia in other countries of the Eastern bloc, for example a small demonstration in Moscow's Red Square on 25 August 1968 including Pavel Litvinov (grandson of Stalin's foreign minister) and Larissa Daniel (wife of the imprisoned Russian novelist). In April 1969 in the Latvian capital Riga, the Jewish student Ilia Rips followed Jan Palach in setting herself on fire. In Poland the repression in Czechoslovakia stimulated student protests, but also strengthened the repressive authorities. Among Eastern European army units engaged in the invasion of Czechoslovakia there were some problems too. They had been led to believe that they were defending the country against West German or American invaders, and some of them were withdrawn because their reliability was in question, especially, it seems, that of Hungarian units in Slovakia. The attitude of many Czechs and Slovaks to the Russians changed, from a rather pro-Russian one to a stance of sullen acquiescence.

Never again would it be possible to maintain that communism rested on popular consent, on the laws and lessons of history, or indeed on the legitimacy of reform efforts. Zdeněk Mlynář, one of the party's leading reformers, recalled ten years later how, on 21 August 1968, Red Army soldiers burst into a meeting of Czechoslovak party leaders and lined up behind each one of them: '... at such a moment one's concept of socialism moves to last place. But at the same time you know that it has a direct connection of some sort with the automatic weapon pointing at your back.' At least as painful was that many who had been among the loudest enthusiasts for Dubček were a few months later among the most enthusiastic purgers and 'normalisers'. Mlynář observed that 'it was only after the

---

[155] Milan Šimečka, *Obnovení Pořádku* (Bratislava, 1984 — in *samizdat*); Milan Simecka, *The Restoration of Order: The Normalization of Czechoslovakia, 1969-1976* (London, 1984).
[156] Judt, *Postwar*, pp. 444-446.

Prague Spring of 1968 that one began to see who was who.'[157] The Czechoslovak tragedy was deeply symbolic, marking a turning point in the history of communism.[158] Communist authoritarian collectivism could not be reformed or be made compatible with democratic pluralism. Perhaps it is true that the soul of communism died in Czechoslovakia in August 1968.

Conclusions

When we compare the Czechoslovak regime crisis of 1968 with the problems of the authoritarian regime in Portugal, we see that the aspect of internal elite disunity was more important in Czechoslovakia. In the 1960s the Czechoslovak Communist party contained several political factions of shifting strength and influence. The party's reformers were divided in a moderate and a radical group, and there was also a conservative wing which opposed many of the reforms from the outset. A part of the moderate reformers and even some of the initially most enthusiastic ones began to have growing doubts about the reform project after mid-1968. This was partly because the momentum of political developments in Czechoslovakia seemed to be spinning out of control, and partly because it became increasingly clear that Moscow wanted the reform process to stop. The 'external' factor of the power of the Soviet Union within the context of the Cold War division of Europe was obviously a crucial reason why the liberalisation policy was bound to fail. The growing

---

[157] Zdeněk Mlynář, *Night Frost in Prague: The End of Humane Socialism* (New York, 1980), quoted in Judt, *Postwar*, p. 447. See for another critical evaluation of the liberalisation period Jiří Pehe (ed.), *The Prague Spring: A Mixed Legacy* (New York, 1988). For reflections on the significance of 1968 in Slovakia, see Miroslav Londák and Elena Londáková, 'Slovakia within Czechoslovakia from 1945 to 1989', in Miroslav Londák, Slavomír Michálek and Peter Weiss (eds.), *Slovakia: A European Story* (Bratislava, 2016), pp. 52-61; Miroslav Londák and Stanislav Sikora (eds.), *Rok 1968 a jeho miesto v našich dejinách* (Bratislava, 2009); Stanislav Sikora, 'Charakteristika "socializmu s ľudskou tvárou"', in Miroslav Londák (ed.), *Rok 1968. Eto vaše delo* (Bratislava, 2008).

[158] As Lonnie Johnson observes, 1968 was a turning point in a number of respects, including the abandoning of Marxism by East European dissidents and the final rupture between the Soviet Union and most Western European communist parties; see Lonnie R. Johnson, *Central Europe: Enemies, Neighbours, Friends* (3rd ed., New York/Oxford, 2011), p. 252.

voice of non-communist opposition forces in Czechoslovakia made the situation even more complex. Apart from the party reformers, there were increasingly active groups of students, artists and intellectuals, but also Catholics, alongside autonomously acting groups of workers and alternative political organisations including the Social Democrats. Some of these had already existed in embryonic form, and were now using the expanding political and social space provided by the radicalising reform process. The emergence of all sorts of publications, civic activities, and competing political and cultural initiatives was proof of the great potential of Czechoslovak democracy. One very important aspect of this was the articulation of the Slovak national issue, which cried out for a just solution.

We have seen that in Portugal in the 1960s similar groups to those in Czechoslovakia began to form an opposition: independent Leftists and workers, critical Catholics, and students and intellectuals (including lawyers). This was of great significance because in Portugal there was less elite disunity than in Czechoslovakia. There were some examples of internal friction and crisis phenomena within the ruling oligarchy, but these did not assume the same proportions as the crisis of the political elite in Czechoslovakia. Particularly important in Portugal was the role of progressive Catholics, and if it were argued that the Catholic Church was itself a part of the ruling elite, this Catholic opposition could of course be interpreted as a prime example of an internal elite crisis—especially in the case of bishops. But the Church was too hierarchical and all-embracing to be reduced to any specific group, with increasingly critical Catholic intellectuals and parish pastors occupying a rather different position in society than High Church officials. As in Czechoslovakia, university students and certain groups of intellectuals constituted another category of opposition elements, which is not surprising given the historic role of intellectual groups in Europe. The role of Leftist and worker organisations is not easy to define, because there were different political groups, with the Portuguese communists representing a political orientation that was not shared by socialists or progressive Catholics. As in Czechoslovakia, 'external' factors influenced the situation in Portugal, in this case especially the policies of the Vatican as well as NATO and the

African colonial crisis. But the context and dynamics were different because the Vatican and progressive organisations in various NATO countries criticised the authoritarian regime and its colonial wars, while the wars themselves played a crucial part in undoing the regime.

The political dynamics of Portugal and Czechoslovakia also differed in other respects. Although both authoritarian regimes survived the crisis of '1968', Portugal belonged to a category of nations which benefited from the wave of democratisation in the 1970s. The difference between Salazar and Caetano was possibly smaller than the difference between Novotný and the genuine reformer Dubček, or indeed between Dubček and the 'normaliser' Husák. But despite Czechoslovakia's desire for freedom, the ability of monolithic Soviet communism to survive for another two decades proved decisive for her fate. Therefore, the Czechs and Slovaks had to wait until 1989, a year of deepening crisis in Eastern Europe and the Soviet Union itself, for 'their' authoritarian regime to collapse.

8. Slovakia and Portugal 1989-1993: changing political cultures and communist movements compared

The 'fall of the Berlin Wall' — or rather the removal of the Iron Curtain and of the communist regimes in Eastern Europe — was a turning-point in European history. It marked the beginning of a new phase in the history of the Slovaks, the Czechs, the Hungarians, and other East-Central European nations, and also prepared the foundations for an independent Slovak Republic as from 1 January 1993. The construction of a post-totalitarian, democratic political culture proved to be more difficult than many observers had expected, perhaps especially in Slovakia with its weakly developed civil society and fragmented political spectrum.

One way to analyse Slovakia's political culture after 1989 and in the early 1990s is to look at the role of the communists and post-communists. The post-communist Party of the Democratic Left, the main successor to the former ruling Communist Party, was more viable than the re-founded orthodox Communist Party of Slovakia, which did not succeed in becoming more than a sect. However, an examination of the ideas and the mentality of its members and supporters provides us with some interesting insights about the 'worldview' of a part of the Slovak population. It also shows that, from a psychological and ideological point of view, the communist movement was a sectarian phenomenon, comparable to a church or religious sect. It is, perhaps, on this level that a comparison with the Portuguese Communist Party could and should be made. An undiluted communist worldview may have become a marginal phenomenon in both countries and across Europe, but this does not mean that it completely disappeared. It also amalgamated more visibly with other ideological elements and radical tendencies — or re-emphasised such tendencies, for instance a defensive isolationism — and thus experienced a partial transformation in political and ideological terms. All of this does not change, but rather confirms the fact that the early 1990s witnessed a weakening of the attractions of the classical communist movement as well as substantial changes in the political cultures of Slovakia and Portugal.

The Portuguese scene

How did the Portuguese Communist Party react to the disappearance of the communist regimes in Eastern Europe in October-December 1989? First and foremost, the PCP refused to acknowledge that the old Marxist-Leninist ideology had become obsolete. It also tried to postpone defining its position as long as possible. This had to do with the existence of internal disagreements within the party and confusion and uncertainty about what to do next, that is, in terms of a survival strategy. The policy of perestroika in the Soviet Union had already caused problems for the party in the preceding years, with the leadership remaining vague and ambivalent in its response. But Alvaro Cunhal and his supporters were forced by the growing internal unrest and criticism by intellectual and other party representatives, and by the increase in the number of outspoken critics of the old principles of 'democratic centralism' and Marxism-Leninism, to organise an extraordinary party congress in May 1990. Here they managed to keep the upper hand and to exclude the most serious critics from attending. José Luis Judas for example, a communist trade union leader, was not admitted to the congress and therefore presented some critical theses at a separate press conference. Judas attributed the failure of 'existing socialism' to a lack of democracy at all levels. He also criticised the PCP's internal hierarchical organisation, the limited information available to the membership, the system of democratic centralism, and the fact that the ageing and rigid Cunhal still had not been substituted as party leader.

Nevertheless, at the May 1990 congress some minor political changes were adopted on the initiative of the party leaders, who thus hoped to calm the situation. Indeed, five 'weaknesses' of the former Eastern European regimes were identified. The first of these was the excessive political centralism and its tendency to take arbitrary and repressive decisions; the second, the severe limitations on political democracy and the rights of citizens; third, the suffocating bureaucracy which led to the stagnation of the productive forces; fourth, the negative consequences of the authoritarian nature of the party; and fifth, the imposition of Marxism-Leninism as a dogmatic State doctrine. Crucial, however, was the PCP's contention that the crisis in the Soviet Union and Eastern Europe had emerged, not because the communist project itself had naturally led to this, but because official party policies had failed to conform to the original fundamental goals and orientation of the communist project. It was admitted that the PCP had failed to appreciate how severe the situation had become, but it was also maintained that the PCP itself was not affected by similar errors and weaknesses.

Thus, the PCP reaffirmed its commitment to the 'communist ideal', in spite of the failure and collapse of socialism in Eastern Europe. This also continued to include full commitment to the principles of Marxism-Leninism and democratic centralism. The party acknowledged and criticised weaknesses and mistakes, but managed to leave the essential core of communist ideology and hierarchical party organisation intact. Following the congress of May 1990 various critics of party policy and party culture were expelled, or decided to resign. The congress was meant to end the debate on the collapse of the socialist regimes and renovation of the party. The failed military coup in the Soviet Union of 19 August 1991 was even defended and supported by the PCP. This appeared to show that the party had always opposed the reforms of Gorbachev. As with the Soviet invasion of Czechoslovakia in 1968, support for the coup placed the PCP within the vanguard of the most conservative communist forces. This led again to heavy criticism of the party in Portugal and to a new wave of resignations.

However, Cunhal and the party leadership quickly recuperated from this crisis and from the renewed demands for fundamental changes in the PCP. The party went on the counter-attack, justified its support for the coup, criticised capitalist restoration in the Soviet Union, and labelled Boris Yeltsin reactionary and anti-democratic. The coup was explained as an attempt to halt the counter-revolutionary process that had developed during perestroika, a desperate attempt to salvage the socialist character of the Soviet Union. During the Portuguese parliamentary election campaign in

October 1991, Carlos Carvalhas, now the second man in the party hierarchy, declared that the events in the Soviet Union had a greater impact upon the intellectuals than upon 'the masses'.

But in the end, the PCP suffered a major defeat, losing one third of its electorate compared with the previous election in 1987 (and more than half when compared with the election of 1983). For the first time the party's election result fell below 10 per cent of the national vote, having declined from 18 per cent in 1983 to 8.8 per cent in 1991. The decrease in party membership may have been slightly less than one third of the total. Nevertheless, the electoral defeat did not make the PCP more self-critical. The losses were blamed on the recent events in the Soviet Union and the way the media had used them against the party, but also on the fact that the Socialist Party refused to form an alliance with the PCP. After the elections the last remaining critics within the party were expelled. In 1993 Alvaro Cunhal finally retired as secretary-general of the party, being replaced by Carlos Carvalhas. A majority of the party continued to insist that the struggle for a 'socialist transformation of society' was their historic objective.

Did the survival of the orthodox PCP reflect in any way the stability or even the rigidity of Portuguese political culture and the party-political landscape? It would seem it did to some extent. Of course, the party was a peculiar phenomenon and the expression of a sectarian 'anti-systemic' tradition, but precisely this, perhaps, was also a part of the broader socio-cultural pattern. The gradual decline of the PCP's traditional social base in sections of the urban and rural working classes as a result of the modernisation of Portuguese economy and society and Portugal's integration in the European Community (1986) had begun to affect the party, but as yet only marginally. The changes in political culture and traditional leftist idealism following the end of the Eastern bloc hit Portugal as well, but perhaps less so than elsewhere. If anything, they have made the PCP more defensive and more determined to survive. The party tried to isolate itself from the effects of the break-up of world communism, maintaining the loyalty of its membership by reaffirming their identity as communists and strengthening its sub-cultural and sectarian dimension. This also convinced many of the more critical party members to hold on to their membership, as if in a fundamental act of loyalty and identity-confirmation. The party's traditional values and the 'communist ideal' were re-emphasised, including — because of the disappearance of most socialist states — a reduced level of international 'solidarity' (such as with Cuba and 'the Palestinians'). Perhaps more interesting, isolationism and patriotism became more significant features of the PCP's repertoire. This also included an 'anti-imperialist' rhetoric — some authors speak of the PCP's 'Third-World mentality' — that seemed to place Portugal in a non-European context. Articulating a form of Portuguese patriotism was potentially a way to attract new voters and to prove the continuing relevance of the party and its programme. For declining communist movements, emphasising national identity is possibly a way to survive.

Were the changes in Portuguese political culture after 1989 superficial? Perhaps 'de-ideologisation', ideological persistence, and communist-nationalist ideological hybridisation were all features of the post-1989 political landscape in Europe, in Portugal, and in Slovakia.[159] Focusing on the Slovak situation may help to elucidate this complex question.

The Slovak scene

As already mentioned, in Slovakia after 1989 the old communist party effectively split up in a post-communist party styling itself the Party of the Democratic Left (SDL) and an orthodox communist minority movement who re-founded the Slovak Communist Party. The SDL developed into a 'neo-Social Democratic' party, which was neither wedded to the Social Democratic tradition nor able to convince the electorate to support its new orientation. At a later stage it was competed out of existence by Robert Fico's more populist and nationalist version of post-communist 'neo-Social Democracy'. As far as the years 1989-1993 are concerned, and in order to facilitate a

---

[159] Our analysis is mainly based on Maria Teresa Patrício and Alan David Stoleroff, 'The Portuguese Communist Party: *Perestroika* and its Aftermath', in Martin J. Bull and Paul M. Heywood (eds.), *West European Communist Parties after the Revolutions of 1989* (London, 1994), pp. 90-118. See for other literature essay no. 7.

comparison with the PCP, it may be more relevant and rewarding to focus on the Slovak orthodox communist group, especially on their worldview, ideological rhetoric, and evaluation of the post-communist situation. This undertaking is made easier by the published memoirs of a representative of the Slovak conservative communists, Ján Zelinka.[160] By looking at these memoirs, we can identify some typical topics illustrating both the changes and the continuity in the post-communist mental frame and the political culture of Slovakia. We will note the persistence of communist ideology and world-interpretation, but also the acknowledgement of the need for communists to respond to the changes that had been taking place in Czechoslovakia and the wider world.

Ján Zelinka, born in west Slovakia in 1922, is a good example of a Slovak communist who remained loyal to the old communist idea and ideal after 1989. In his memoirs, written between 1990 and 1998 and published in Bratislava in 2000, he shows himself to be a man adhering to a conservative and doctrinaire ideological orientation without being entirely uncritical of certain aspects of the old political system. Zelinka was a scientist, a biochemist, and neither a man familiar with the more complicated historical and political questions of twentieth-century Europe nor a party careerist. Precisely because of this, he may serve as an example of the more educated and sincere type of Slovak party member who regarded 'real existing socialism' as an essentially positive system and who did not really understand or appreciate what pluralist democracy was supposed to be. For people like Zelinka, and probably even more for less educated or politically indifferent people in the former Czechoslovak Socialist Republic, basic social security, stability, and political predictability were of supreme importance. These values could be combined with a specific kind of conservatism, traditionalism, and isolationism, and with suspicion of 'capitalism' and 'the West'.

Zelinka describes how, by 1989, the reform policy of Gorbachev began to have some belated influence in Czechoslovakia and

---

[160] Ján Zelinka, *Od romantiky k vede a politike (Spomienky, udalosti, úvahy)* (Bratislava, 2000). There is not much literature like these memoirs by Zelinka.

how in Slovakia they were expecting to see some liberalisation on the domestic political scene as well, albeit 'in the spirit of our own national and democratic traditions'.[161] While he does not explain what these traditions are, he seems to acknowledge that a certain measure of democratisation was necessary. On the other hand, he writes that before 1989 only 'a few disaffected intellectuals' (a group that obviously does not include himself, but consists of the Slovak equivalents of Václav Havel) were interested in openly criticising the system. He also suggests that Slovakia's 'Velvet Revolution' of November 1989 was something that was imported from outside, from Prague and the West; that the propaganda of the Western media was largely responsible for it; and that 'money' from the West must have played 'a decisive role'. In other words, he did not believe that the Slovak people themselves were interested in putting an end to the socialist system. Those who founded the anti-communist platform 'Public against Violence' were doing so in an attempt to survive as political actors, he writes, and 'the Slovaks understood much earlier than the Czechs that the "Velvet Revolution" had deceived them', that is, that their lives would become worse rather than better.

For Zelinka, it was all a cheat; he did not believe that the Velvet Revolution could ever have brought the Slovaks anything positive. The revolution 'was not the expression of social tension' or serious disaffection, but rather endangered what in his view were the advantages of the old order: 'The socialist system of the Czecho-Slovak type—however imperfect—ensured to the great mass of the population permanent employment, social security, a decent level of existence in the form of inexpensive foodstuffs, housing, possibilities to travel and cultural activities, free education and health care, and social care at old age.'[162] This probably sums up rather well why people like Zelinka continued to support the communist system, which they believed benefited the common people and the working class. There may have been a lack of freedom of expression and the like, but it was hardly worth mentioning.

---

[161] Ibid., p. 459.
[162] Ibid., p. 463.

According to Zelinka, 'the spirit of the November revolt was formed by students and artists, two groups of the population with little experience of real life.'[163] But it also appeared, 'as in the year 1968, that the working class was not immune to the counter-revolution either', especially because it was not led by its 'natural', determined leaders. Zelinka thus identifies two crucial problems: the inordinate influence of marginal intellectual people on the revolutionary (or counter-revolutionary) events, and the bad qualities and characteristics of many of the official political and working-class leaders. Indeed, many party bureaucrats — theoretically the leaders of the working class — 'proved not to have the qualities required for their posts'. He acknowledges that there were many 'careerists' in the party, and that the events of 1989 showed how significant the difference between real communists and official party functionaries was. After the revolution (or 'revolt'), he writes, it became necessary and inevitable to separate the former from the latter, in an attempt to fight back against the forces that wanted to undo — in fact, were undoing — the achievements of their 'socialist development'.[164] This was not easy, and even in the Slovak Academy of Sciences, the place where Zelinka worked as a scientist, there was a 'hysterical atmosphere' in which the anti-communists were taking over.[165] This process started in November 1989 and went on unabated during the following months.

However, within the Slovak Communist Party (KSS) — which during communism had existed as a quasi-autonomous organisation parallel to the centralist Czechoslovak Communist Party — a 'Platform for Communist Renewal' (PCR) was formed to oppose the transformation of the party into a more Social Democratic-type of political party. According to Zelinka, the Platform was the only political movement at that moment which in its initial programme based itself 'on the progressive message of our history, on the tradition of the struggle against fascism, on the message of the Slovak National Uprising', and so on.[166]

---

[163] Ibid., p. 464.
[164] Ibid., p. 466.
[165] Ibid., p. 473.
[166] Ibid., p. 483.

This old ideological and anti-fascist phraseology and the references to the Second World War were not exactly what mattered most during the months and years of post-communist democratisation after November 1989, but it gives us an indication of the mental frame of the orthodox communists. As in the past, they sought to legitimise themselves by representing communism as the indispensable political and moral core of the 'anti-fascist tradition', a 'tradition' they tried to monopolise—as if there had been no non-communist anti-fascists—and which they had always cultivated in an attempt to make both others and themselves believe that this was more important than the raw reality of their dictatorial regime. The communists' 'anti-fascism' was, in addition to their claim of ensuring social security, a major pillar of their propaganda. Without the constant references to the Second World War there was apparently no legitimacy for old-style communism, but the communist interpretation of the War was ideologically manipulated. A third argument of the orthodox communists besides 'social security' and 'anti-fascism' was that some of the old communist leaders, including Gustav Husák, had been sincere men. He and other party leaders had worked for many years for the common good, and according to Zelinka, 'it was generally known that they did not enrich themselves', as one of the first programmatic documents of the Platform explicitly claimed.[167]

The majority of the old Communist Party in Slovakia founded within a year the Party of the Democratic Left, a name that Zelinka found abhorrent. The Platform evolved during 1990-1991 into the Union of Slovak Communists, and in August 1992 it fused with a second orthodox communist group to form a new Communist Party of Slovakia. In the elections in 1992 the orthodox communists won less than 1 per cent of the Slovak vote, but in the late 1990s support for the party increased and in 2002 the KSS won 6.32 per cent of the vote and eleven seats in the Slovak parliament. Thereafter, however, support for the party declined again sharply. Fico's party Smer replaced the SDL and managed to attract many old communist voters with both a social-populist and a national-

---

[167] Ibid., p. 485.

populist programme. Indeed, as in Portugal, the national aspect was an important basis of party rhetoric and propaganda. Both the communists and Smer portrayed Slovakia as a state that must be social and sovereign, even if the reality—including the reality of Fico's policies during his terms as prime minister—was somewhat different. But despite its disappearance as a viable political force, the communists' worldview is still alive among a section of the Slovak population and left-wing voters.

About the authors

Zuzana Poláčková
Currently she is working as a senior research fellow at the Institute of History of the Slovak Academy of Sciences (SAS). In the past she worked at the Institute of Political Science of the SAS, she lectured at Comenius University in Bratislava and at Webster University in St. Louis, USA. In her research activity, she systematically addresses three main problem areas: the foreign policy of Czechoslovakia in the 20th century in a European context, the issues of nationalism, ethnic minorities and migration, and social democracy and its role in the history of the 20th century.

Pieter C. van Duin
Currently he works as an independent historian, focusing on problems of ethnicity and social conflict. Pieter van Duin studied history and philosophy at the University of Leiden. He specialised in social and economic history as well as European colonial history. In the past he worked at the University of Leiden and the University of Cape Town in South Africa. He is an honorary fellow of the International Institute of Social History in Amsterdam, the Netherlands.

ibidem.eu